THE DEMISE OF
Loss and Extinc

)
be
date

Maintaining the natural diversity of the countless species on Earth is of fundamental importance for the continued existence of life on this planet. Nevertheless, ecosystems are being destroyed, as the cultivation of land for agriculture, industry and housing is intensified and oceans continue to be exploited. *The Demise of Diversity: Loss and Extinction* deals with biodiversity on this planet and the vital importance of sustaining it – nothing less than the future of life on Earth.

Josef H. Reichholf was Professor for Nature Conservation at the Technical University of Munich. In 2007 he was awarded the Sigmund Freud Prize for his accessible scientific prose and for many years he was a board member of the German World Wide Fund for Nature.

Our addresses on the Internet:
www.the-sustainability-project.com
www.forum-fuer-verantwortung.de
[English version available]

THE DEMISE OF DIVERSITY
Loss and Extinction

JOSEF H. REICHHOLF

Translated by Sandra Lustig and Michael Dills

Klaus Wiegandt, General Editor

HAUS PUBLISHING

First published in Great Britain in 2009 by
Haus Publishing Ltd
70 Cadogan Place
London SW1X 9AH
www.hauspublishing.com

Originally published as: *Ende der Artenvielfalt? Gefährdung und Vernichtung von Biodiversität* by Josef H. Reichholf

Copyright © 2007 Fischer Taschenbuch Verlag in der S. Fischer Verlag GmbH, Frankfurt am Main

English translation copyright © Sandra Lustig and Michael Dills 2009

The moral right of the author has been asserted

A CIP catalogue record for this book
is available from the British Library

ISBN 978-1-906598-15-0

Typeset in Sabon by MacGuru Ltd
Printed in Dubai by Oriental Press

Mixed Sources
Product group from well-managed forests and other controlled sources
www.fsc.org Cert no. CU-COC-809367
© 1996 Forest Stewardship Council
FSC

Haus Publishing believes in the importance of a sustainable future for our planet. This book is printed on paper produced in accordance with the standards of sustainability set out and monitored by the FSC. The printer holds chain of custody.

Contents

Editor's Foreword

Sustainability Project

Sales of the German-language edition of this series have exceeded all expectations. The positive media response has been encouraging, too. Both of these positive responses demonstrate that the series addresses the right topics in a language that is easily understood by the general reader. The combination of thematic breadth and scientifically astute, yet generally accessible writing, is particularly important as I believe it to be a vital prerequisite for smoothing the way to a sustainable society by turning knowledge into action. After all, I am not a scientist myself; my background is in business.

A few months ago, shortly after the first volumes had been published, we received suggestions from neighboring countries in Europe recommending that an English-language edition would reach a far larger readership. Books dealing with global challenges, they said, require global action brought about by informed debate amongst as large an audience as possible. When delegates from India, China, and Pakistan voiced similar concerns at an international conference my mind was made up. Dedicated individuals such as Lester R. Brown and Jonathan Porritt deserve credit for bringing the concept of sustainability to the attention of the general public, I am convinced that this series can give the discourse about sustainability something new.

Two years have passed since I wrote the foreword to the initial German edition. During this time, unsustainable developments on our planet have come to our attention in ever more dramatic ways. The price of oil has nearly tripled; the value of industrial metals has risen exponentially and, quite unexpectedly, the costs of staple foods such as corn, rice, and wheat have reached all-time highs. Around the globe, people are increasingly concerned that the pressure caused by these drastic price increases will lead to serious destabilization in China, India, Indonesia, Vietnam, and Malaysia, the world's key developing regions.

The frequency and intensity of natural disasters brought on by global warming have continued to increase. Many regions of our Earth are experiencing prolonged droughts, with subsequent shortages of drinking water and the destruction of entire harvests. In other parts of the world, typhoons and hurricanes are causing massive flooding and inflicting immeasurable suffering.

The turbulence in the world's financial markets, triggered by the US sub-prime mortgage crisis, has only added to these woes. It has affected every country and made clear just how unscrupulous and sometimes irresponsible speculation has become in today's financial world. The expectation of exorbitant short-term rates of return on capital investments led to complex and obscure financial engineering. Coupled with a reckless willingness to take risks everyone involved seemingly lost track of the situation. How else can blue chip companies incur multi-billion dollar losses? If central banks had not come to the rescue with dramatic steps to back up their currencies, the world's economy would have collapsed. It was only in these circumstances that the use of public monies could be justified. It is therefore imperative to prevent a repeat of speculation with short-term capital on such a gigantic scale.

Taken together, these developments have at least significantly improved the readiness for a debate on sustainability. Many more are now aware that our wasteful use of natural resources and energy have serious consequences, and not only for future generations.

Two years ago, who would have dared to hope that WalMart, the world's largest retailer, would initiate a dialog about sustainability with its customers and promise to put the results into practice? Who would have considered it possible that CNN would start a series "Going Green?" Every day, more and more businesses worldwide announce that they are putting the topic of sustainability at the core of their strategic considerations. Let us use this momentum to try and make sure that these positive developments are not a flash in the pan, but a solid part of our necessary discourse within civic society.

However, we cannot achieve sustainable development through a multitude of individual adjustments. We are facing the challenge of critical fundamental questioning of our lifestyle and consumption and patterns of production. We must grapple with the complexity of the entire earth system in a forward-looking and precautionary manner, and not focus solely on topics such as energy and climate change.

The authors of these twelve books examine the consequences of our destructive interference in the Earth ecosystem from different perspectives. They point out that we still have plenty of opportunities to shape a sustainable future. If we want to achieve this, however, it is imperative that we use the information we have as a basis for systematic action, guided by the principles of sustainable development. If the step from knowledge to action is not only to be taken, but also to succeed, we need to offer comprehensive education to all, with the foundation in early childhood. The central issues of the future must be anchored firmly in school curricula, and no university student should be permitted to graduate without having completed a general course on sustainable development. Everyday opportunities for action must be made clear to us all – young and old. Only then can we begin to think critically about our lifestyles and make positive changes in the direction of sustainability. We need to show the business community the way to sustainable development via a responsible attitude to consumption, and become active within our sphere of influence as opinion leaders.

For this reason, my foundation *Forum für Verantwortung*, the ASKO EUROPA-FOUNDATION, and the European Academy Otzenhausen have joined forces to produce educational materials on the future of the Earth to accompany the twelve books developed at the renowned Wuppertal Institute for Climate, Environment and Energy. We are setting up an extensive program of seminars, and the initial results are very promising. The success of our initiative "Encouraging Sustainability," which has now been awarded the status of an official project of the UN Decade "Education for Sustainable Development," confirms the public's great interest in, and demand for, well-founded information.

I would like to thank the authors for their additional effort to update all their information and put the contents of their original volumes in a more global context. My special thanks goes to the translators, who submitted themselves to a strict timetable, and to Annette Maas for coordinating the Sustainability Project. I am grateful for the expert editorial advice of Amy Irvine and the Haus Publishing editorial team for not losing track of the "3600-page-work."

Taking Action – Out of Insight and Responsibility

"We were on our way to becoming gods, supreme beings who could create a second world, using the natural world only as building blocks for our new creation."

This warning by the psychoanalyst and social philosopher Erich Fromm is to be found in *To Have or to Be?* (1976). It aptly expresses the dilemma in which we find ourselves as a result of our scientific-technical orientation.

The original intention of submitting to nature in order to make use of it ("knowledge is power") evolved into subjugating nature in order to exploit it. We have left the earlier successful path with its many advances and are now on the wrong track, a path of danger with incalculable risks. The greatest danger stems from the unshakable faith of the overwhelming majority of politicians and business leaders in unlimited economic growth which, together with limitless technological innovation, is supposed to provide solutions to all the challenges of the present and the future.

For decades now, scientists have been warning of this collision course with nature. As early as 1983, the United Nations founded the World Commission on Environment and Development which published the Brundtland Report in 1987. Under the title *Our Common Future*, it presented a concept that could save mankind from catastrophe and help to find the way back to a responsible way of life, the concept of long-term environmentally sustainable use of resources. "Sustainability," as used in the Brundtland Report, means "development that meets the needs of the present without compromising the ability of future generations to meet their own needs."

Despite many efforts, this guiding principle for ecologically, economically, and socially sustainable action has unfortunately not yet become the reality it can, indeed must, become. I believe the reason for this is that civil societies have not yet been sufficiently informed and mobilized.

Forum für Verantwortung

Against this background, and in the light of ever more warnings and scientific results, I decided to take on a societal responsibility with my foundation. I would like to contribute to the expansion of public discourse about sustainable development which is absolutely essential. It is my desire to provide a large number of people with facts and contextual knowledge on the subject of sustainability, and to show alternative options for future action.

After all, the principle of "sustainable development" alone is insufficient to change current patterns of living and economic practices. It does provide some orientation, but it has to be negotiated in concrete terms within society and then implemented in patterns of behavior. A democratic society seriously seeking to reorient itself towards future viability must rely on critical, creative individuals capable of both discussion and action. For this reason, life-long learning, from childhood to old age, is a necessary precondition for realizing sustainable development. The practical implementation of the ecological, economic, and social goals of a sustainability strategy in economic policy requires people able to reflect, innovate and recognize potentials for structural change and learn to use them in the best interests of society.

It is not enough for individuals to be merely "concerned." On the contrary, it is necessary to understand the scientific background and interconnections in order to have access to them and be able to develop them in discussions that lead in the right direction. Only in this way can the ability to make appropriate judgments emerge, and this is a prerequisite for responsible action.

The essential condition for this is presentation of both the facts and the theories within whose framework possible courses of action are visible in a manner that is both appropriate to the subject matter and comprehensible. Then, people will be able to use them to guide their personal behavior.

In order to move towards this goal, I asked renowned scientists to present in a generally understandable way the state of research and the possible options on twelve important topics in the area of sustainable development in the series "*Forum für Verantwortung*." All those involved in this project are in agreement that there is no alternative to a united path of all societies towards sustainability:

- *Our Planet: How Much More Can Earth Take?* (Jill Jäger)
- *Energy: The World's Race for Resources in the 21st Century* (Hermann-Joseph Wagner)
- *Our Threatened Oceans* (Stefan Rahmstorf and Katherine Richardson)
- *Water Resources: Efficient, Sustainable and Equitable Use* (Wolfram Mauser)
- *The Earth: Natural Resources and Human Intervention* (Friedrich Schmidt-Bleek)
- *Overcrowded World? Global Population and International Migration* (Rainer Münz and Albert F. Reiterer)
- *Feeding the Planet: Environmental Protection through Sustainable Agriculture* (Klaus Hahlbrock)
- *Costing the Earth? Perspectives on Sustainable Development* (Bernd Meyer)
- *The New Plagues: Pandemics and Poverty in a Globalized World* (Stefan Kaufmann)

- *Climate Change: The Point of No Return* (Mojib Latif)
- *The Demise of Diversity: Loss and Extinction* (Josef H Reichholf)
- *Building a New World Order: Sustainable Policies for the Future* (Harald Müller)

The public debate

What gives me the courage to carry out this project and the optimism that I will reach civil societies in this way, and possibly provide an impetus for change?

For one thing, I have observed that, because of the number and severity of natural disasters in recent years, people have become more sensitive concerning questions of how we treat the Earth. For another, there are scarcely any books on the market that cover in language comprehensible to civil society the broad spectrum of comprehensive sustainable development in an integrated manner.

When I began to structure my ideas and the prerequisites for a public discourse on sustainability in 2004, I could not foresee that by the time the first books of the series were published, the general public would have come to perceive at least climate change and energy as topics of great concern. I believe this occurred especially as a result of the following events:

First, the United States witnessed the devastation of New Orleans in August 2005 by Hurricane Katrina, and the anarchy following in the wake of this disaster.

Second, in 2006, Al Gore began his information campaign on climate change and wastage of energy, culminating in his film *An Inconvenient Truth*, which has made an impression on a wide audience of all age groups around the world.

Third, the 700-page Stern Report, commissioned by the British government, published in 2007 by the former Chief Economist of the World Bank Nicholas Stern in collaboration with other economists, was a wake-up call for politicians and business leaders alike. This report makes clear how extensive the damage to the global economy will be if we continue with "business as usual" and do not take vigorous steps to halt climate change. At the same time, the report demonstrates that we could finance countermeasures for just one-tenth of the cost of the probable damage, and could limit average global warming to 2° C – if we only took action.

Fourth, the most recent IPCC report, published in early 2007, was met by especially intense media interest, and therefore also received considerable public attention. It laid bare as never before how serious the situation is, and called for drastic action against climate change.

Last, but not least, the exceptional commitment of a number of billionaires such as Bill Gates, Warren Buffett, George Soros, and Richard Branson as well as Bill Clinton's work to "save the world" is impressing people around the globe and deserves mention here.

An important task for the authors of our twelve-volume series was to provide appropriate steps towards sustainable development in their particular subject area. In this context, we must always be aware that successful transition to this type of economic, ecological, and social development on our planet cannot succeed immediately, but will require many decades. Today, there are still no sure formulae for the most successful long-term path. A large number of scientists and even more innovative entrepreneurs and managers will have to use their creativity and dynamism to solve the great challenges. Nonetheless, even today, we can discern the first clear goals we must reach in order to avert a looming catastrophe. And billions of consumers around the world can use their daily purchasing decisions to help both ease and significantly accelerate the economy's transition to sustainable development – provided the political framework is there. In addition, from a global perspective, billions of citizens have the opportunity to mark out the political "guide rails" in a democratic way via their parliaments.

The most important insight currently shared by the scientific, political, and economic communities is that our resource-intensive Western model of prosperity (enjoyed today by one billion people) cannot be extended to another five billion or, by 2050, at least eight billion people. That would go far beyond the biophysical capacity of the planet. This realization is not in dispute. At issue, however, are the consequences we need to draw from it.

If we want to avoid serious conflicts between nations, the industrialized countries must reduce their consumption of resources by more than the developing and threshold countries increase theirs. In the future, all countries must achieve the same level of consumption. Only then will we be able to create the necessary ecological room for maneuver in order to ensure an appropriate level of prosperity for developing and threshold countries.

To avoid a dramatic loss of prosperity in the West during this long-term process of adaptation, the transition from high to low resource use, that is, to an ecological market economy, must be set in motion quickly.

On the other hand, the threshold and developing countries must commit themselves to getting their population growth under control within the foreseeable future. The twenty-year Programme of Action adopted by the United Nations International Conference on Population and Development in Cairo in 1994 must be implemented with stronger support from the industrialized nations.

If humankind does not succeed in drastically improving resource and energy efficiency and reducing population growth in a sustainable manner – we should remind ourselves of the United Nations forecast that population growth will come to a halt only at the end of this century, with a world population of eleven to twelve billion – then we run the real risk of developing eco-dictatorships. In the words of Ernst Ulrich von Weizsäcker: "States will be sorely tempted to ration limited resources, to micromanage economic activity, and in the interest of the environment to specify from above what citizens may or may not do. 'Quality-of-life' experts might define in an authoritarian way what kind of needs people are permitted to satisfy." (*Earth Politics*, 1989, in English translation: 1994).

It is time

It is time for us to take stock in a fundamental and critical way. We, the public, must decide what kind of future we want. Progress and quality of life is not dependent on year-by-year growth in per capita income alone, nor do we need inexorably growing amounts of goods to satisfy our needs. The short-term goals of our economy, such as maximizing profits and accumulating capital, are major obstacles to sustainable development. We should go back to a more decentralized economy and reduce world trade and the waste of energy associated with it in a targeted fashion. If resources and energy were to cost their "true" prices, the global process of rationalization and labor displacement will be reversed, because cost pressure will be shifted to the areas of materials and energy.

The path to sustainability requires enormous technological innovations. But not everything that is technologically possible has to be put into practice. We should not strive to place all areas of our lives under the dictates of the economic system. Making justice and fairness a reality for everyone is not only a moral and ethical imperative, but is also the most important means of securing world peace in the long term. For this reason, it is essential to place the political relationship between states and peoples on a new basis, a basis with which everyone can identify, not only the most powerful. Without common principles of global governance, sustainability cannot become a reality in any of the fields discussed in this series.

And finally, we must ask whether we humans have the right to reproduce to such an extent that we may reach a population of eleven to twelve billion by the end of this century, laying claim to every square centimeter of our Earth and restricting and destroying the habitats and way of life of all other species to an ever greater degree.

Our future is not predetermined. We ourselves shape it by our actions. We can continue as before, but if we do so, we will put ourselves in the biophysical straitjacket of nature, with possibly disastrous political implications, by the middle of this century. But we also have the opportunity to create a fairer and more viable future for ourselves and for future generations. This requires the commitment of everyone on our planet.

Klaus Wiegandt

Summer 2008

I Introduction

Viewed from space, Earth is a planet of water. The six great continents – Eurasia, Africa, North America, South America, Australia, and Antarctica, as well as many thousands of islands of all sizes – lie surrounded by ocean, which covers some 70 percent of the planet's surface. But it is not solely the blue of the sky as reflected in the water of the oceans, lakes, and rivers that characterizes the Earth. Green also colors the globe, in fine gradations in the sea and in strongly contrasting hues on the land. Although naked rock and sand make up vast expanses of the land's surface, and ice covers Antarctica and large parts of the North Pole region, green dominates much of our planet. It is the color of life. By far the greatest part of life on Earth depends on this green, is nourished by it, and by turns increases or diminishes it. It gave the planet's enveloping air its substantial oxygen content, and before that 'burned' the exposed surface of the earth for many millions of years, until the green itself came out of the sea onto the land and, some half a billion years ago, set a development in motion that we, with great amazement, can call the conquest of the land. We ourselves are one of the many products of this evolution – humans as a biological species.

We could not have come into existence if not for 'nature,' with its abundance of life forms and its productive capacity. We humans do not stand opposite nature. Rather, we are one species among many life forms on earth – without a doubt a tremendously potent one, one with a greater impact than any other that has ever existed. Yet we are not the only species that has fundamentally altered nature. Long before we evolved, there were changes on a massive scale. This was fortunate for us, for without these changes we would not have become what we are. We owe our existence to the rise of plants on land, to the development of forests and grasslands. We need fresh water and we need the animal world, from which our ancestors lived until just a few millennia ago. We require a diversity of plants and the variety of substances contained in them in order to get the necessary range of food and the active agents (vitamins, minerals) in it which our bodies cannot produce. As a biological species humans remained fully integrated in and reliant on nature's diversity over a period of around one hundred fifty thousand years. Yet our genus goes back much further than the type of human we call *Homo sapiens*.

Human development began five to six million years ago in tropical East Africa, where, simultaneously with our most distant ancestors, a great variety of animals developed. A segment of this still exists in the geographical birthplace of humanity – but almost exclusively in nature reserves. These became necessary because humans and the large animals that formed the basis of our existence not only there, but everywhere, can no longer live in balance with each other. This is the core of the problem in the conflict between humans and nature.

Humanity has, in biblical terms, 'subdued the earth' and risen dramatically from the status of a rare species itself threatened with extinction to the planet's absolutely dominant life form, which by now has impacted on and massively altered practically all of nature. The consequence is a far-reaching threat to nature. Its variety of life forms and habitats is dwindling. Species are being killed off, or are dying out unnoticed because we are not aware even of their existence. The interaction of species is itself changing, or is being transformed into entirely different, heretofore nonexistent forms through humans' use of force and energy. Formations, structures, and landscapes that are made and shaped by people are spreading, taking in ever larger portions of the globe. Via fixed road and transport systems, the human world is extending out into the countryside from the cities, from the centers of human settlement of our times, which are unmistakable as artificial formations. Routes by water and air – that is, ones not bound to specific locations – have made the human world a global network. Agricultural tracts have grown to cover seemingly endless expanses of land. Vacation resorts penetrate the wilderness. These forces are joined by the invisible, hidden influences that are present everywhere on the earth.

Nothing on earth remains as it was just a few thousand years ago. No place on the globe remains completely untouched by detectable human influence, no such thing as virgin nature exists. We have only this 'One World.' On it and from it, we and all other species must live – we with them and they with us. Friction is unavoidable. There have already been great losses, and there will be more. Fundamentally it is not a question of whether, but very concretely how, non-human life can survive alongside humanity and how much this will cost in terms of life's diversity. Humans are pressing into all corners of the earth. Wherever we spread out, nature is necessarily pushed back. There can be no romantic 'back to nature.' And the sentimental archiving of 'beautiful species' in zoos and botanical gardens does not offer a true alternative. Humanity will not be able to live from grain and bread alone when this means the ever more radical intervention in nature and brings ever greater losses. And those who do not have to struggle to survive, but can spare even a few moments to reflect on the natural world, cannot but acknowledge that the life that surrounds them has meaning. All peoples and cultures known to humanity have observed and assessed their natural environment. Animals and plants, above all large mammals and birds as well as trees and forests, have been valued, even deified. Nature has also always been used and exploited. Not until our time, however, has that which is a completely normal expression for all life forms, namely to use our environment as well as possible and to multiply as much possible, so exceeded the sustainable. The overuse of nature has become humanity's greatest problem. Use has turned into exploitation – indeed, into rapacious exploitation. Resources are being used to the point of exhaustion, to the point of outright destruction, while the natural world is being overburdened with refuse and toxins and changed in its chemical composition.

The diversity of life on earth is part of the natural resources that, like the water and the soil, the forests and the oceans, comprise the foundation for our life. But unlike natural materials such as water and minerals, coal and petroleum, oxygen and carbon dioxide, which can be counted, measured, weighed, and estimated in their supply, life changes on its own, from within itself. It renews itself, uses the resources that it needs, alters these or produces them 'anew' through processes of transformation that we term 'recycling.' The most important characteristic of life forms is their ability to multiply. Only living things can grow and reproduce, renew themselves and even change, over longer or shorter periods of time. We call the latter evolution. Hence, in considering life on earth, different problems come to the fore than are the focus when assessing water resources, energy conversion or economic parameters. This certainly does not make it any easier to assess life's diversity. On the contrary. It is still not truly accorded value in itself, but as something that seems in large part to be dispensable. Because we have no 'need' for a little beetle which might even become a pest, and we write off flies and other such creatures as useless or dangerous. Because forests consisting of only one or a small handful of tree species produce wood faster than biologically diverse jungles. Because livestock cannot live on the bitter grasses and poisonous herbs of colorful and varied rangeland. Most people want wheat, potatoes, and tobacco, not natural zoos of grasshoppers, crickets, vibrant flowers, and singing birds that produce nothing edible. While some may take pleasure in the lively diversity of the natural world, it is not considered essential by the great majority of the population. Only where our cultural achievements have altered nature does it produce what we need and want from it. The rest of nature is, at best, banished to the museum-like margins that nobody cares about.

Are nature and the protection of nature merely the luxury of the prosperous societies, whose populations are no longer growing but shrinking, and which can therefore afford to decorate 'the great outdoors' with the unnecessary trappings of wealth like a living room? In the face of the rapidly growing world population and the conflicts between rich and poor, and against the background of political and religious tensions and divisions, it may appear pointless to concern ourselves with the preservation of colorful butterflies, or to consider birds with shimmering plumage 'important.' Why is it not enough to get the waters somewhat cleaned up, reduce air pollution, and use the necessary resources sparingly? Good environmental protection, after all, will also preserve a bit of life's diversity. Does the protection of nature as practiced in the West not also mean an all-too-paternalistic stance toward poor, insufficiently developed states? Is it not a continuation of the political and mental colonialism of the past, using the means of our time? Why, in fact, should all the countries at the Earth Summit in Rio de Janeiro

in 1992 have committed themselves to maintaining the variety
of life on earth – its biodiversity – and achieving sustainable
development in harmony with it? Up to now, almost nothing has
come of these efforts. Does this tell us that the call to action was
unconvincing? What would the stakes have to be for us to make
preservation of the diversity of life on earth a priority?

There is no stock explanation. This may be a good thing, as
zealots all too often abuse 'irrefutable' explanations for their
own purposes and exploit prejudices for their own gain. It is
then but a small step to credo and, further, to dogma. In setting
global objectives, dogma would certainly do more harm than
good, and might result in a division into different, ultimately
warring camps. Biodiversity still has the advantage that it does
not carry this dogmatic baggage. Thus we should look more
closely at biodiversity in order to understand what 'diversity' in
nature means, how it comes into being, and what its dwindling
tells us. The advantage of this approach lies in the fact that the
phenomenon of biological diversity is itself extremely varied,
taking very different expressions both within a given region and
globally. Certain areas and countries possess a special, distinguishing biodiversity. Uniqueness offers opportunity for differentiation. When New Zealand adopts the kiwi bird, Australia
the kangaroo, and the United States the bald eagle as national
symbols, we are clearly dealing with special regional features that
are neither arbitrary nor to be found everywhere. Life on earth is
not only highly diverse, but also very unevenly distributed. Additionally, the distribution of the various living things over various
regions brings with it its own history. Tiny islands are home to
one-of-a-kind creatures, and great life forms must by no means
be limited to the great continents. We take for granted that the
same plants and animals will not be found around the world.
How bland such uniformity would be.

2 A Planet Full Of Life

Recording Biodiversity

How many animal species are there in a Central European country like Germany? Surprisingly, this simple question cannot be answered precisely. No comprehensive and current species inventory has yet been taken. At present there is only more or less extensive knowledge about particular groups of animals. There is more information on birds than on any other single group. Considerably less is known about the distribution and abundance of Germany's other animal species. In its 2003 Red List of Threatened Animals of Bavaria the Bavarian Environment Agency published the most comprehensive survey for Central Europe to date. It takes in around 16,000 different animal species, seemingly an immense number. Still, the survey does not come close to accounting for all the species that inhabit Bavaria, but only about half of them. No one person knows them all. For some animal groups, such as beetles, there are specialists who deal with certain subgroups and can precisely identify all the species within them. The flora of Bavaria, on the other hand, has been almost completely recorded. There are far fewer plant than animal species, however. The corresponding Red List of Threatened Vascular Plants of Bavaria, also published in 2003, contains 2,863 species, 656 subspecies, and 88 varieties. Extrapolated to take in all of Central Europe, the number of species would rise to between 3,500 and 4,000 plants, depending on how the area of roughly one million square kilometers was defined. This figure would not include the algae species or the microscopic organisms such as bacteria and viruses. The distinct kingdom of the fungi, with its thousands of species, is also omitted from the Bavarian inventory of its living nature at the turn of the third millennium. Thus these surveys, extensive as they are, still do not yield a comprehensive list of all living species in Bavaria. While Bavaria, at some 70,000 square kilometers, is not an especially large territory, it has been fairly well researched by European standards. For a number of animal groups there is quite exact data. Currently, 187 bird species regularly breed in Bavaria and over a dozen further species do so occasionally. There is a similar number of butterfly species, 172 in all. The moths comprise many more – over 1,000. Additionally, there are more than 2,000 species of microlepidoptera, bringing the full spectrum of butterflies and moths occurring in Bavaria to over 3,200. Lepidoptera specialists therefore have a similar abundance of species to cope with as do experts on Central European plants. In comparison, the ten species of reptiles, twenty amphibians and 80 mammals are decidedly modest in number. They are also better known, including with regard to their incidence and frequency. Yet not well-known enough. This is illustrated by the many problems related to the protection of these groups as well. Why, for example, are populations of lizards and snakes, animals dependent on warmth, not increasing, but instead widely endangered, although the climate is growing warmer?

Species that we know a lot about are those that are conspicuous to us due to their size, their form, or the way they live, or the fact that they cause damage or health problems. Most people can name about as many pests and pathogens as they can other animals and plants. Taken together, all of these well-known species nonetheless make up only a tiny part of the actual bio-diversity that surrounds us. Even large cities, with their gardens and parks, waters and 'vacant' spaces, are so rich in species that nobody knows or could identify them all with certainty. Life is around us, always and everywhere. Living organisms exist where we least expect them, such as in the ice of the polar regions or the rock of the earth's crust. Wherever humans have searched for life on earth, we have found it. It flourishes around the fiery throats of undersea volcanoes far deeper than sunlight can penetrate, drifts on air currents over the highest mountain peaks, sprouts on humans' well-washed skin, and in the foulest sewage pits. We usually do not take notice of the abundance of life that surrounds us. We take the green of the trees for granted as a pleasant back-drop. And where it is missing, we can plant more trees. We listen to the birds' singing, or ignore it once we have grown accustomed to it. When the birds fall silent, we take notice. But the natural world around us is changing. Where sparrows once dominated, we now find blackbirds. The formerly common meadows of colorful flowers have grown rare. We encounter butterflies more typically in the garden than 'out in nature.' Conservationists complain of the declining numbers of many species. The above-mentioned study on the state of the natural world in Bavaria resulted in nearly half (49 %) of the 16,000 animal species and a comparable proportion of the plant species being classified as 'threatened.' What must the state of things be in places where nature has been studied far less than in Central Europe?

What do such findings mean? Is the situation in Bavaria cause for general alarm? Is this a special case or one that is representa-tive for Central Europe? The Red List is produced every ten years. A comparison of that from 2003 with those of earlier decades shows a clear increase in the threat, not the decrease three decades of nature protection efforts might lead us to expect. The more intensive the research, it turns out, the greater the extent of the danger that is revealed. Still, one might think, Bavaria – even all of Central Europe – surely is not that significant for Europe as a whole or for the rest of the world. There is too little here that is unique to this region. The great majority of animal and plant species range far beyond Bavaria, their areas of distribution extending in many cases deep into Asia. And half of the species here are on the safe side. Of the threatened species, it will be possible to preserve many, perhaps even the majority. Protective programs to this end have already been enacted. Nature reserves have been declared in large number. The desire to conserve nature is securely anchored in society. Less poison is being set out to combat undesired species. All songbirds are under protection as endangered species, as are many other animals and plants as well. The great landscapes that spread out to the east still have much more nature than we do here. So the threat to species cannot really be all that drastic, even if Bavaria is representative for all of Germany and Central Europe. Or can it? Caution is in order. How good are the surveys of biodiversity? The mere determination that species exist in greater or lesser numbers tells us nothing about changes, about trends, or about their true endangerment. The current state, even assuming it has been sufficiently investigated, provides nothing more than a snapshot of the present situation. It says nothing about the level of threat or about factors of endangerment or extinction. Rarity can be completely natural, representing no threat at all, or it can mean that in the foreseeable future a species will vanish from the area in question, perhaps even die out entirely. We need to know more than such a stock-taking can tell us.

Changing the focus, then, from the local to the global, we can ask how the situation looks for the biodiversity of the earth as a whole. The first Earth Summit, in Rio de Janeiro in 1992, declared the preservation of global biodiversity one of the chief aims of the community of states, along with sustainable development. When we speak of biodiversity, what exactly do we mean?

What Is Biodiversity?

Biodiversity refers to the natural variety comprised by living things. It encompasses, in the common view, not only the different species of plants, animals and microbes, but also the habitats which they form and the 'inner diversity' which organisms carry in their genetic make-up. The species themselves certainly make up the core of biodiversity, as they both determine the manifestations of life as an expression of form-giving external forces and carry forward and maintain inner, genetic variety. In this way, out of individual trees a forest takes shape with conditions of temperature and moisture different to those in treeless but otherwise comparable terrain. A forest of just one species of tree with greater genetic uniformity is more susceptible to pathogens or outbreaks of insect populations than a mixed forest consisting of different species and genetically more diverse trees. Rare species that are small and have little influence will hardly make themselves noticed in comparison with more abundant ones that strongly influence natural processes. Accordingly, specialists must often search for years just to find all the rare species of butterflies, beetles, or other insects in a forest, while a small number of related species can defoliate entire forests in a short time. On the other hand, such insect pests can more easily be fought when they possess little, as opposed to greater, genetic diversity.

The inner diversity that makes each human being a unique individual is our best collective insurance against plagues and other pandemics. Similarly, how we humans alter the environment depends not solely on what we are as a biological species, but also on what we do and how we intervene in nature. Biological variety, or biodiversity, can be best understood if we transpose the conditions of our own existence 'out into nature.' There, however, we are not dealing with one species, as in our own case, but with a plethora of different ones. Knowing and being able to appraise these species is central to understanding biodiversity. As we have not been able to identify all of the planet's species thus far, and very probably will not be able to record all biodiversity in the foreseeable future, we must settle for an appraisal of representative parts of it.

These are the more conspicuous animals and plants, such as the birds and the trees and a number of other forms of life, whereas the great majority of inconspicuous species remain so, because we cannot see them or cannot identify them easily enough. However, in recording biodiversity we must not be content to, for example, find all of the existing bird species and determine the utility value of all tree species. It has never been only the obvious varieties that have proven especially important or beneficial. Rather, it is often the small differences that determine whether an organism is benign or poses a danger. Some differences are so subtle as to make identification difficult even for experts. And much more simply, a species may remain unknown because nobody has yet investigated it or because it is new to science. What do we mean by the term 'species,' anyway?

Species And Diversity Of Species

Species means the blackbird in the garden, the daisy in the meadow, the sparrow on the roof and the cockchafer on the tree. This is one possible answer to the question of what species are.

But whereas the first two organisms are in fact species, this is not the case with the sparrow or the cockchafer. Each of these in fact designates two Central European species, the house sparrow (English sparrow) and the Eurasian tree sparrow and the common and forest cockchafer. Further sparrow and cock-chafer species exist in Southern Europe and bordering regions. Finch denotes a bird group that includes numerous species, trout likewise designates a range of different species, and so on. While there are very good field guides for the identification of all the birds of Europe or North America, there are discrepancies between these books due to changing views as to what constitutes a species. For example, as recently as the late 1990s the water pipit, a well-known small bird, was divided into two different species, the water pipit and the rock pipit. A number of such re-designations were made among known species in the nineteenth century. The tree creeper, for example, was found to comprise both the short-toed tree creeper and the Eurasian tree creeper. The long-tailed tit with the all-white head, meanwhile, was found to be of the same species as the Western and Southern European variety bearing broad dark stripes on its head, thus nullifying the prior division into two separate species.

One might consider such 'problems' to be entertaining games for specialists. After all, what is the significance to people generally of whether two little birds belong to the same species or two different ones? Similarly, why should the ornithologically debated question of the distinction between the European herring gull of the North and Baltic Sea coasts and the very similar gulls found in the Mediterranean and the Black Sea region be of consequence to our well-being as humans? At some point the experts will arrive at a consensus and the field guides will be emended accordingly. Yet what in some cases could be dismissed as irrelevant can suddenly take on great importance – for example, when it comes to the question of whether these large gulls can (also) carry and transmit the dangerous H_5N_1 type of avian influenza virus. This depends on their place of origin, possible close contact between members of the three gull species, and their sharing, as synanthropic species, of human habitat – for instance, in cities, where they might readily come into contact with people. To determine the paths by which pathogens spread, we must know the species well enough and investigate the routes of their migrations. The confusion around the spread of bird flu in Europe in the winter of 2005/2006 was the result of the state authorities' lack of knowledge of the migratory patterns of the affected water birds, which in some cases led them to declare the wrong areas off limits.

A much greater problem arises with regard to the possible renewed spread of malaria. Mosquitoes that are killed as a precaution may not be carriers of the pathogen, and therefore harmless. Or they may be life-threatening, as in the case of the malaria-transmitting genus *Anopheles*. This type is widespread in Europe, including parts of Germany and the Nordic regions. The possibility that they may soon carry and transmit the malaria pathogen again is considered a real danger. The ability to differentiate between benign common mosquitoes and those that can transmit malaria thus is critical to precautionary meas-ures. This applies also to ticks as disease carriers, and generally to insects that can cause severe economic damage. The impor-tance of precise knowledge becomes painfully clear when, for example, such damage is due to the population explosion of a particular species that has been mistaken for a very similar but harmless one. Here, the obvious is not enough. At the end of May in years of good spring weather, trees in parks and forests are often cocooned in silvery white and eaten bare by caterpillars of a small ermine moth. The resulting tree-skeletons could surely be assumed to be doomed to die. This is not always the case, however. If the affected tree is a bird cherry, it soon sends out new shoots and produces a new generation of foliage, and the masses of caterpillars of this bird cherry-specialized moth do not return until the following year. Combating the pests with poison or special bacteria, such as *Bacillus thuringiensis*, would do more harm than good, as the tree and the moth are adapted to one another. The 'obvious damage' is far less severe than it appears. But if the caterpillar of a closely related and very similar small ermine moth attacks apple trees, it can indeed have a negative impact on the fruit harvest.

Matters become much more difficult when even exact microscopic observation is no longer sufficient to answer the question: 'Harmless germ or dangerous infection?' An incorrect diagnosis or the wrong medicine can have fatal consequences. This is where inner, genetic diversity comes in. It is not the species of a pathogen that becomes resistant that has changed, but rather its genetic capacity. Conversely, the genetic diversity within the affected species is crucial to its defense against germs.

Thus the species stands right in the middle between the internal – genetics – and the external – ecology. The species is the biological unit that makes possible free and successful reproduction. Organisms that belong to the same species can reproduce together. Those belonging to different species cannot – or can do so only in a restricted and incomplete way. All humans belong to one single species, significant differences in appearance notwithstanding. That we differ from our nearest relatives, the chimpanzees, by only a good one percent in our genetic make-up is nonetheless more than sufficient to separate these great apes from the human species. Modern molecular genetics is able to determine ('measure') the genetic differences. It can therefore also be helpful in delineating between two species whose representatives normally would not meet because they live too far from one another.

In genetic terms, the American beaver and the European beaver are two distinct species, and where populations of American and European beavers are settled in close proximity, they hardly mix. In contrast, wolves of North America and Eurasia behave completely as a unified species, demonstrating a readiness to interbreed. Their offspring are unrestrictedly fertile and remain wolves. The cross-breeding of horse and donkey, on the other hand, produces mules or hinnies, depending on which is the father and which the mother. They cannot reproduce.

Even the long separation of different populations within a species – dating as far back as the Ice Age in some cases – does not always give rise to two independent species. Often, however, the changeable climate has rapidly created new species due to changed living conditions. A precise definition of the term 'species' necessarily rests on much theory and logic, but frequently fails when it runs up against the realities of nature, in which conditions are often fluid rather than fixed. From this arises, all by itself, the special significance of genetic diversity. Within the species, it is desirable that this be preserved as much as possible or further expanded. But species are alterable. Their alteration gives us evolution. This is only mentioned herein passing, because the problem of genetic diversity requires later treatment in greater depth, in order for important aspects of the protection of species to become understandable.

What is the basic issue here? Knowing the different species is essential to dealing with them effectively. This has been the case since time immemorial for the larger and smaller predators that have posed a threat to humans, as well as for both poisonous and medicinal plants. And it is especially true with regard to food, which can be dangerous if ill-chosen or spoiled by other organisms. Telling the useful from the harmful has always been so crucial to human survival that it still fundamentally shapes our basic attitudes and behavior toward our environment. Between these two poles lies that which is 'uninteresting' – uninteresting because it is not (yet) of use to us or no longer harmful, or because it is unknown. The latter is of special importance. By far the greatest part of the existing variety of life is not yet known. In this respect, the position of humanity in the larger natural world is like that of the individual person within humanity. We are personally familiar with only a small number of other people. Of these, we know a yet smaller handful well enough that we can 'assess' them with any accuracy. We have a sense that the vast majority of those with whom we are not acquainted are, by virtue of our shared humanity, not barbarians. Though it can be argued that any one individual does not 'need' this great number of others, especially when they live far from our own place of dwelling, such an attitude is frowned upon, and for good reason. All people are accorded the same human value. Together we form humanity's inviolable unity, which takes in all varieties of appearance, way of life and way of thinking. Every individual represents an unrepeatable uniqueness. Our use of the expression 'one of a kind' is no coincidence.

In the same way, every other organism is a unique individual within its own species and, at the same time, distinguishable from all other species. The vast variety of life is thus analogous to human diversity, but in a much greater dimension. If we assume that diversity is a general characteristic of life, the answers to many of the questions arising in the sections and chapters to follow take shape of their own accord. Whatever question we set out to answer, however, it is important that we do not judge prematurely. Especially when it comes to assigning value, judgments can quickly become biases. Yet we do not even know the starting conditions. While Europe, North America, and few other regions have been fairly thoroughly studied in an effort to inventory the species that inhabit them, this is not at all the case for the much greater part of the earth. For this reason, there is as yet no useful answer to the next question.

How Many Species Live On The Earth?

At present, and presumably for the foreseeable future, this apparently simple question cannot be answered. All that is certain is that the earlier assumption of two to three million species was far too low, even though this order of magnitude seemed well-founded based on the state of knowledge of the 1970s. At that time, some 1.5 million animal and plant species had been scientifically described and definitively named. Specialists thought they could roughly estimate the number of species they would have to work through to take a virtually complete inventory of their respective animal and plant groups. In well-researched animal groups such as birds, they did not expect to discover a large number of 'new' species. Among little-studied animals and several plant families, the estimated figure was accordingly higher. An approximate doubling of the number of known species seemed plausible. The end of the recording of the planet's biodiversity, the global stock-taking, appeared within reach. Two and a half centuries had been needed to sight the first 'half' of the total spectrum. The second would require perhaps a few decades. And more research funding.

These resources were provided, and they were put to use where scientists expected to discover new species: high in the tree canopy of the tropical rainforests. The Smithsonian Institution in the United States strengthened its tropical research in the 1970s when it became clear that a rapid destruction of the tropical forests had begun. The breakthrough to a literally new dimension came with research carried out in the crowns of trees in Panama by the then young tropical biologist Terry Erwin. In the late 1970s Erwin investigated the insect life of individual tree species in the tropical rainforest on the island of Barro Colorado in the Panama Canal. He discovered so many previously unknown beetle species that he began to reassess the calculations. This led to a stunning result: in the crowns of one tree species, *Luehea seemanni*, he determined that there were around 1,100 species of beetle, 160 of which were specialized for this tree species alone. Since beetles make up around 40 percent of the total spectrum of insect species, Erwin estimated that there must be roughly 400 different insect species exclusive to *Luehea seemanni*. As two-thirds of the insect species inhabit the canopy, the remaining third – the trunk and root dwellers – raised the number of insects specialized for *Luehea seemanni* to 600. Multiplied by the 50,000-plus distinct tree species in the tropical forest, the possible number of tropical forest insect species alone came to some 30 million.

Similar conclusions were reached in studies of the rainforests of Peru and Borneo. Such rough calculations are undoubtedly flawed, as the assumptions that underlie them cannot be easily justified. Accordingly, Terry Erwin's estimates were strenuously disputed. Other calculations that included microbial organisms arrived at a magnitude of 100 million species. Yet even conservative estimates put the number at ten million species or more, or five times that assumed before 1980. The correct figure likely lies somewhere between ten and 100 million species. In the last twenty-five years, however, a lack of sufficient funding for research of the Earth's biodiversity has thwarted progress towards answering this question. There are also too few specialists capable of identifying species. A vast number would obviously have to be described for the first time, as barely more than 1.8 million species have been scientifically recorded up to now. This would mean that for every known species in the tropical forests, there would be four to five unknown ones – or ten times that number, should the higher estimates be correct. At the current state of the available global capacity for determining and recording species diversity, it would take millennia to gain a reasonable overview.

Thus, for the time being, the earth's wealth of species must remain a great unknown. Unlike an iceberg, whose overall size can be judged based on the tip that rises above the water, the earth's biodiversity cannot be so simply gauged. We know enough about only a few groups of animals and plants to be able to generate sufficiently exact figures. The best known of these, the birds, comprise just under 10,000 species. With over 1,200 threatened bird species – or one in eight – there is a very high degree of endangerment globally. The 16,000 threatened species contained in the Red Lists of the International Union for Conservation of Nature (IUCN) surely make up, in numbers, only a tiny fraction of the planet's total biodiversity. But these are chiefly species of birds, mammals, reptiles and amphibians, as well as fish and other large, conspicuous – and perhaps also important – species. The numbers must be placed in the proper context so as not to convey a false impression or foster the conclusion that, among the millions of surely existent yet unknown species, the 16,000 listed as threatened are insignificant. A look at the estimable or known numbers of species of different groups of organisms (Table 1) helps put this in perspective.

Mammals	4000	endangered 1180
Birds	9800	endangered 1200
Reptiles	4000	
Amphibians	3500	
Fish	25–30 000	
Butterflies	140 000	
Mollusks (snails/mussels/squids)	120 000	Insects 2–30 (50) million?
Plants	300 000	

Table I Approximate number of species in different groups (according to Dobson 1997 and various later estimates)

Tropical Species Richness

Geographically speaking, species richness is distributed very unevenly. Biodiversity increases greatly from the polar latitudes to the equator. Global diversity is concentrated in the tropics, giving us a simple basic relationship: the warmer habitats are, the richer they are in species. Higher life forms are rare on the polar icecaps. Those that can be found there at all seek out the ice only at certain times for particular purposes, as in the case of penguins that brood and rear their young in the Antarctic. Like the polar bears and seals of the Arctic, these birds must secure their food from the sea. The rainforests of the tropics, on the other hand, are so rich in species that they constitute the great unknown in the assessment of global biodiversity. Figure 1 shows how strongly the diversity of species rises with increasing proximity to the inner tropics. Closer inspection reveals that even very small tropical countries like Costa Rica (an area smaller than Bavaria) are home to a greater number of bird species than are the giant continental expanses of North America.

For the extensively studied bird world, the increase in species

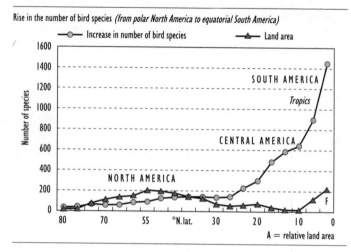

Rise in the number of bird species *(from polar North America to equatorial South America)*

Figure 1   Increase in the number of bird species (⊚) from arctic North
America (80° N. latitude) through Central America to the
equator in South America (Amazonia)

The triangles (▲) indicate the comparative land area at the respective latitudes.
The narrow Central American isthmus is far richer in species than all parts of
North America

richness toward the inner tropics can be represented continuously. For most other groups of animals and plants, however,
only sections can be compared (Figure 2).

The species density (number of species per 100 square kilometers) of butterflies in Costa Rica alone is more than twenty
times that in Northwestern Europe. Central and South America
generally exhibit a greater density of butterfly species than does
Africa (Figure 3).

Day-flying butterflies, however, make up only quite a small
part of the overall variety of lepidoptera. In Germany, the
almost 200 day-flying species constitute only about 6 percent of

Density of butterfly species (species/100km²)

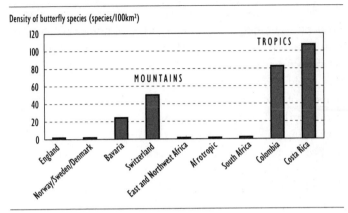

Figure 2   Density of butterfly species (species per 100 km²) in various
            regions of Europe, East and Northwest Africa, South Africa,
            South and Central America

Diversity of butterflies

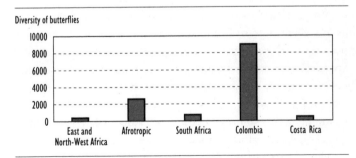

Figure 3   Diversity of butterfly species in Africa (East and Northwest
            Africa, tropical Africa south of the Sahara, and South Africa)
            compared to Colombia and Costa Rica
            Colombia has an extremely high species diversity, with over 9000 butterfly
            species

the more than 3,500 species of moths and microlepidoptera, a proportion similar to that found in the combined territory of Europe and extra-tropical Asia. Transposed to Colombia, this relationship suggests that up to 120,000 species of microlepidoptera could be expected to occur there, almost as many as the number of lepidoptera species of all kinds known today in the entire world. These extrapolations for lepidoptera thus offer a supporting point of comparison for Terry Erwin's calculations for beetles in Panama. And support comes from other quarters as well: wherever more thorough investigations have been carried out, 'tropical records' have been reported for virtually all other insect groups.

This is true also of the plant world. The most species-rich family, the orchids, occurs mainly in the tropics. Among tree species there is a similar tropical preponderance. Some 2,400 different tree species inhabit Venezuela, compared to just over forty in Northwestern Europe. Many tropical species are so difficult to identify that, even among trees, further new discoveries are expected. Thus even for the large and noticeable species, the recording of species diversity in the tropics cannot be regarded as anywhere close to complete. In recent years there have even been new discoveries of larger mammals. A number of areas that are accessible only with difficulty – notably the border region between China, Vietnam, Cambodia, and the northern edges of Burma and Thailand, as well as remote mountain valleys in the Colombian, Peruvian, and Ecuadoran Andes and in New Guinea – likely hold surprises in store.

The tropics clearly also provide the main range for frogs, snakes, lizards, and turtles, all groups in which the great majority of species cannot survive in cooler climes. Only the birds and mammals, which generate their own body heat, could have advantages in extra-tropical habitats. But among these groups, too, the largest part of the spectrum of species lives in the tropics: over 500 mammal species alone in tropical Central and South America, or more than double the number found in all of Europe. Among birds, the number of species is at least three times as high for the tropical Americas as for Europe. The species richness in mammals and birds in Africa and Southeast Asia surpasses that of the bordering extra-tropical regions by a similar magnitude. The species density in the archipelagos of Southeast Asia considerably exceeds even that of Amazonia. This finding points up the role – as well as the problem – of islands as habitat. For as a general rule, counter to what might be expected given the fabulous richness of life in the tropics, a large part of these island species are rare or very rare. High species richness in no way also means high security. Indeed, the opposite is almost always true: the higher the number of species in a region, the more threatened nature is there. At sea as on land: in the oceans, it is the tropical coral reefs that support the greatest species diversity, not the productive temperate and cold marine regions. There is a quite unexpected inverse biological relationship between 'productivity' and biological variety: diversity is a consequence of scarcity of essential resources, while abundance, the result of 'productivity,' leads to a smaller number of dominant species.

The Ecology Of Diversity

The early European explorers who journeyed to the tropical world of the Americas or Southeast Asia were astonished by the abundance of species and life forms they encountered there. Their descriptions shaped Europeans' image of tropical luxuriance. At the turn of the nineteenth century Alexander von Humboldt, deeply impressed by his *Travels to the Equinoctial*

Regions of the New Continent, that is, to the inner tropics of the Americas (1799–1804), concluded that only an especially favorable, a very productive nature could bring forth such variety. The trees of tropical forests reach high into the air toward the light. Many are hung with vines. Orchids, ferns and other epiphytes grow on their branches. Colorful butterflies flutter among them. The forest is filled with a concert of myriad birds, accompanied by the clamor of cicadas, crickets and other insects. At every turn, Humboldt and his companion, the botanist Aimé Bonpland, encountered new, completely unknown species of animals and plants. They noted their sightings and collected samples, attempting to further penetrate this tropical treasure trove. In the three centuries that had passed since Europeans had discovered and colonized the New World, monkeys and parrots, hummingbirds, and other curiosities had found their way to Europe. But for all their novelty, these life forms provoked little more than amazement. Even crop plants like the potato, corn, tobacco, the tomato, and plant products such as cocoa originally had only a limited impact. The Europeans coveted gold and silver, and they were busy building up their colonial power. The native populations of the Americas were decimated or wiped out altogether. The slave trade thrived. Most tropical diseases were originally absent from the Americas; they were introduced by Europeans and the African slaves. Not until Europe's early industrial economic boom did interest grow in the other natural resources found in the tropics of the Americas. Europeans set about to survey and map the earth accurately enough that their ships could find their intended destinations. Charles Darwin's great journey on the British surveying vessel *Beagle* served this primary purpose as well; the gathering of knowledge of the fauna and flora of the distant continents was of secondary concern.

Yet other interests also became apparent. The Europeans

looked to the regions they had 'discovered' and occupied with an eye to permanent colonization – by European settlers, of course, on whose behalf expeditions increasingly sought suitable land. The scientific investigation of the tropical flora and fauna was undertaken against the background of these other, more urgent interests. Hence Alexander von Humboldt's reflection that the unexplored tropical rainforests, inhabited only by a sparse population of 'savages,' must hold the last great land reserve for (European) humanity. For where nature flourished so luxuriantly, it should also prove fertile for humans. This fallacy has held sway right up to the present – with disastrous consequences for the people and nature of the tropics.

Two clear discoveries that could have been considered reliable indicators as to the nature of the tropical Americas went unheeded. The first widely known finding was made by Humboldt himself when he traveled, first, the Orinoco River, which joins with a northern tributary of the Amazon in the interior of the continent, and, later, the Andean highlands. In the cold heights of the Andes, three to four thousand meters above sea level, the great culture of the highland Indians still lived, spread over an extensive contiguous area. These were the descendants of Indian peoples who had been ruled by the Incas at the time of the conquest of South America. In contrast to the austerity of these high altitudes, the warm, wet lowlands of the Amazon and Orinoco were only very thinly and fragmentarily settled by Indians. The lowland Indians lived in small groups on the material level of the Stone Age. The minimal mark they had made on the great endless forests was, for researchers such as Humboldt, completely imperceptible.

But why should people – native Indians as well as European colonists who had arrived in the last three centuries – have favored the high expanses and coastal regions at the neglect of this largest tropical rainforest on earth, which was so full of timber and water and had a warm climate uninterrupted by winter or substantial dry periods over the course of the year? In the austere and cold Andean highlands there were cities with populations numbering in the tens of thousands and a permanent advanced civilization. Amazonia, on the other hand, had only temporary settlements of people who lived in huts and in simple villages that were not sustained over long periods.

The situation was very similar in the tropics of Central America, where the advanced civilizations existed in the highlands of Mexico and neighboring countries, while the tropical lowlands of the Yucatán saw only limited settlement – alongside the ruins of the ancient Mayan culture, overgrown by the jungle. To the south of the giant forests of Amazonia, the Jesuits had, with an Indian population in Paraguay and northern Argentina, built up a flourishing 'state.' This was perceived by Brazil and Argentina (and the Vatican) as too threatening and so was destroyed. At the same time the Brazilians, who had primarily settled along the Atlantic coast, saw the hinterland as useless and showed little interest in penetrating into it, where, as they perceived it, Indians lived like animals of the forest. Not until the end of the nineteenth and beginning of the twentieth century did these forests become the focus of suddenly global interest, because a tree grew there whose sap was indispensable in the production of tires for motor vehicles: rubber from *Hevea brasiliensis*.

In short, in Amazonia as well as along the Orinoco and Colombia's Magdalena River, original settlement and the subsequent European colonization both largely avoided the inner-tropical forests, although they were by no means full of disease or dangerous animals. The fever epidemics, as, for example, during the construction of the Panama Canal, were imports from the Old World and not the effect of a hostile natural world in the newly discovered tropics. In the tropics of the Americas, the Indians were able to live naked, unconcerned about illness. Many of them revered the powerful jaguar, yet in their huts and hammocks had little cause to fear him. Giant snakes that drop out of trees onto people were invented for sensation-seeking readers, so that the great forests could be written off as a 'green hell.'

However, the ecological significance of these realities was not recognized. The researchers also did not respond to the second, more specific signal for more than 100 years. As early as 1864, the British explorer and collector Henry Bates, in his travel account *The Naturalist on the River Amazons*, had clearly stated that in the center of Amazonia (in the vicinity of the modern-day city of Manaus) it was easier to catch ten butterflies of different species than ten of the same. With this observation almost one-and-a-half centuries ago, Bates pointed out that many animal and plant species of the tropics are rare or even very rare. Although the variety of butterflies and birds in the Amazon is colorful, only a small number of individual species are in fact common. The vast majority are hard to find. More recent research – near the end of the twentieth century, when scientists had begun to study the phenomenon of tropical rarity more closely – showed, for example, that, of the more than 200 species of birds that occur in a nature reserve in central Amazonia near the metropolis of Manaus, almost all are so rare that there is less than one pair per square kilometer. Most of these are small, like European songbirds. Some, such as the hummingbirds, are tiny. They could be expected to be correspondingly more abundant, since at such diminutive size they require only small territories.

In a Central European riparian forest of near-natural conditions, on the Danube or the Elbe, for example, there are 40 to 50 different bird species per square kilometer. Together they

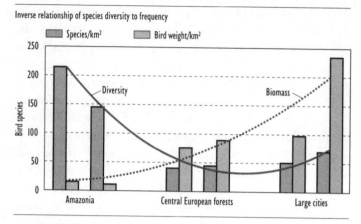

Inverse relationship of species diversity to frequency

Figure 4   While Amazonia, the earth's most species-rich tropical forest, is home to many different bird species, the frequency of most of these is low

Central European forests, like other forests at climatically temperate latitudes, have considerably fewer species, but the birds occur at much higher frequency. The greatest frequency, however, is found in large cities

number between 1,200 and 1,550 breeding pairs. When the males sing at the beginning of the breeding season in the spring, a loud and truly polyphonic choir fills the forest. In Amazonia, four to five times this number of bird species amounts to only 360 to 540 breeding pairs per square kilometer, or one-third to one-fourth of the Central European frequency. Translated into weight, the difference is even more astonishing. Taking all species together, the Amazon's bird world is represented by 11 to 16 kilograms live-weight per square kilometer, while that of Central Europe weighs in at 90 to 100 kilograms or more. Topping the rankings, however, are not the riparian forests, which are known for their richness of species, but the big cities, with up to 380 kilograms live-weight per square kilometer (in Hamburg). (Further comparisons can be found in Reichholf, 2004). These and many other studies show that species richness and frequency are inversely related to each other. The more species there are, the less common they are on average, and vice versa (Figure 4).

Why is this the case? Why are the tropics so rich in species in nearly all groups of organisms, be they plants, land animals, or marine animals? And why should species richness, and biodiversity generally, be coupled with rarity and with scarcity of resources?

The Development Of Species Variety

To understand biodiversity, we must know how it arose and how it is sustained. Until recently, tropical nature was believed to inherently favor the formation of new species. While this view retained its place in ecology textbooks right into the latter decades of the twentieth century, it is certainly not valid generally, if at all. The plethora of species found in the tropics and in other species-rich regions exists not because nature there is so productive, but because it yields so few usable surpluses. An example from our Central European region illustrates why the formerly accepted explanation of tropical biodiversity does not hold.

Here, the greatest range of flowers, herbs, and grasses occurs in grasslands or heathlands that are nutrient-poor and sparsely vegetated. The variety is indeed striking. Butterflies of the most diverse species flutter above the meadows. There are crickets and wild bees and many other insects – so many that hardly a single specialist knows or could identify them all. However, the diversity of species disappears if the nutrient-poor grassland is heavily fertilized, which recently has been common practice, especially after the consolidation of farmland. This diversity is replaced by the spread of a monotonous, uniform green that is composed of just a small number of different grasses and herbs, but which grows more densely with greater fertilization. Butterflies and other insects become increasingly rare and, with the exception of a few species, eventually disappear.

This process has been thoroughly studied and is easily understandable: the fertilization favors a small number of plant species. These prosper and eventually crowd out most of their more sensitive neighbors. Where, prior to fertilization, variety prevailed, monotony sets in – a highly productive monotony that brings far higher yields than the unfertilized meadow. Due to the ample supply of plant nutrients, multiple cuttings of the grass each year or more intensive grazing by livestock are possible. A chief aim of agricultural land use has always been to promote the growth of the few 'useful' species and keep their many possible competitors at bay. In grasslands and farmlands, and usually also in forests, monocultures deliver far greater short-term output than do polycultures. The more species the mix includes, that is, the greater the species diversity, the smaller the yield. An especially species-rich and mature tropical rainforest in which the trees no longer become taller, but are replaced by new growth at the rate they die off and decompose, ceases to produce a surplus – a 'usable surplus' that could be harvested. All of the smallest opportunities and all waste that is produced are further utilized by organisms in the most diverse ways. In this state the forest, viewed from outside, appears highly stable, yet inside is in a constant state of transformation. None of the trees or other species gains greater advantage or predominance through competition. The scarcity that has come about due to the use of even the smallest surpluses also prevents the strong species from competing out the weaker ones.

The variety of trees in the tropical rainforest, where hundreds of different species grow in each square kilometer, is analogous to the hundreds of different plant species in the nutrient-poor grasslands of Europe. Here, too, no species succeeds in spreading out long-term and dominating the others. And since the vast majority of them differ from one another slightly in their specific needs, they can exist together in these species-rich communities. And not merely 'exist'! Such conditions hold the potential of very particular forms of adaptation. Slight differences in the availability of certain minerals in the soil, such as magnesium, iron, phosphates, or cobalt, can have an effect on selection. This means that these environmental conditions give some species and, even more, some genetic combinations within a species, advantages or disadvantages. Every species carries an inner (genetic) diversity. Were this not the case, plant and animal breeding never would have come about. Just how great, how almost unbelievably great, this genetic diversity is can be seen in the spectrum of cultivated forms of dogs and cats, pigeons and chickens, decorative flowers and agricultural crops, as well as fruit and vegetable varieties. Long before the discovery of the genome and the principles of heredity, animal and plant breeders exploited this inner diversity to breed 'new' traits not originally expressed in a species.

More than all of his observations in nature, it was this active selective breeding, which 'produces' such new traits by taking advantage of randomly expressed characteristics, that set Charles Darwin on the right track in his investigations in the mid-nineteenth century. What he found in nature he called natural selection, borrowing the term from active selection as practiced by breeders. Darwin recognized the purpose of heredity and the consequences it has for the variability of species. Without the benefit of the knowledge later gained in the area of genes and heredity, he had discovered one of the chief mechanisms of evolution. He now also understood why, on the many islands he visited in the course of his world circumnavigation on the *Beagle*, he almost always found species that bore a resemblance to, yet were recognizably different from those on the mainland or other islands in the vicinity. Another factor had to be added to inner diversity, or the variability of species, in order to activate a process of selection that was not intended or controlled by humans. In the islands, Darwin found the key to this, and found the explanation for breeders' success in producing such amazing differences in relatively few generations. They isolated the animals and plants they were breeding from other members of the same species, and they used small stocks, not large numbers.

Such conditions arise in nature when low productivity of the habitat allows only small populations of individual species and when these populations (must) live isolated from one another on true islands where they arrived at some point in time. Or because individual populations of species become geographically isolated due to scarcity of their required resources, even if no natural barriers such as water, mountains, or desert lie between them. The other species that also survive are sufficient to limit these populations. This can be observed directly when we examine a nutrient-poor meadow of abundant flowers. Some, perhaps even many, plant species are distributed in island-like patterns within the meadow. Only a few species are more or less evenly distributed. These are the common species, whereas those that occur in island-like 'isolation' are the rarer ones.

If this isolation lasts for a sufficiently long time, variations in these species occur completely on their own. Certain characteristics or new alterations (mutations) in the genetic material become concentrated. Others disappear because the local conditions are slightly different than elsewhere. Local populations of the species are formed initially. If these are not 'replenished' by the general population, their genetic make-up changes so much over time that a subspecies emerges. Often, though not always (yet clearly determinable using modern methods of molecular genetics), the subspecies takes on external characteristics which obviously set it apart from the species from which it arose. In the continued absence of genetic exchange with other populations of the same species through inward and outward migration, that is if, in the terminology of the field, there is no subsequent 'gene flow,' the difference gradually becomes so great that the subspecies becomes a species of its own. As a subspecies, it can in principle still crossbreed with the main species or its other subspecies, yielding offspring that are again able to reproduce with members of their own kind. Once a 'good species' has developed – that is, a reproductive barrier has arisen – this is no longer possible. Or, such interbreeding leads to major and apparent defects or deficiencies. Horses and donkeys are such true ('good') species, even though they can crossbreed with one another, as the mules or hinnies that this produces are infertile.

In such large animals as horses and donkeys this is all readily apparent. Under natural conditions the crossing of wild horses and wild donkeys could almost never occur. In nature many different species live in general proximity to one another or share the same territory, but there are barriers that protect against and counteract a great mixing of species. This phenomenon is more strongly developed among animals than among plants. Externally, many insects are so extremely similar that it takes a true specialist to determine what species they belong to. And in some cases, even the specialists cannot be sure. Butterfly and beetle researchers often have to use a 'genital preparation' to conclusively identify certain species. This is because in many insects the male and female reproductive organs (must) correspond to each other like a key to a lock. Subtle differences in scents and pheromones are more important than appearance, which can vary greatly.

Among many plants, on the other hand, there are hybridizations between species which lead to new 'habits,' or growth forms, and to different emphases in the utilization of their habitats. A doubling or quadrupling of the total genotype (chromosome set) can occur. These forms are called polyploids. Thus plant species cannot be as clearly differentiated from one another as is normally the case with animals. We will return to the question of the function of species diversity in a different context when we discuss the significance of genetic diversity for human beings.

From this explanation it emerges that the formation of (new) species is a process that requires time. How much time depends on various factors, such as the body size and reproductive rate of the original species. Elephants take much longer to establish new generations and new populations than do mice, mice longer than many insects. Medical research is engaged in a perpetual battle against the fastest organisms of all, the viruses and bacteria, because these change their genetic makeup so rapidly, giving rise to new lines with altered virulence (pathogenicity). The current concern with regard to the swift mutation of the H5N1 avian flu virus is a case in point, as is the heretofore unsuccessful struggle against the highly changeable malaria pathogen, for which science has so far not been able to develop a vaccine. Evolution is constantly taking place all around us. Especially in pathogens and parasites, it progresses very quickly, while in other areas it is so slow that it can only be recognized at the geological time scale of millions of years, by means of fossil sequences.

However, the isolation of a group of related organisms is always the most important prerequisite for a change that brings something new and leads to the formation of species. The smaller an isolated yet viable population is, the faster this occurs. A small population of a single animal or plant species almost inevitably lacks parts of the genetic endowment of the species as a whole. This can result in a defect or an advantage as other previously hidden or suppressed traits become more strongly expressed. The genetic material (genome) contains genes numbering in the thousands to tens of thousands. Individual variations number in the millions. No single organism can possibly carry all traits of the species, just as no one person can carry all the genetic material found in humanity as a whole. Small groups thus always form a subgroup also in genetic terms. Their average differs more or less strongly from the average of the species. But where the possibilities for variation become smaller and natural selection comes into play more strongly due to the prevalence of special conditions, the formation of species also progresses more rapidly.

New developments thus usually arise in (small) marginal populations that have been isolated for sufficiently long periods. On islands this development accelerates, as the odds of mating with descendants of the main population, which generally inhabits the mainland, become smaller with decreasing size of the island itself and with increasing distance from the mainland. As a result, new species arise more quickly on islands than on the mainland, where large, constantly mixing populations dominate and buffer each other against changes. Additionally, the living conditions on islands are, as a rule, different from those on the mainland. We now have three fundamental prerequisites for the formation of species and the emergence of high levels of diversity: (1) variation, (2) a small local population, and (3) separation (isolation) from the main population. These are reinforced by (4) the duration of the isolation and (5) improved opportunities for development because of changed living conditions. Point

4 is readily apparent; if the period of isolation is too short for the differences to become great enough, renewed contact with the main population again leads to mixing and to the disappearance of many of the special traits that have arisen through selection in isolation. Point 5, on the other hand, must be examined more closely. A population on an island will develop little independence if the living conditions, especially with regard to the other animal and plant species in its habitat, hardly differ from those on the mainland. But if the colonized island is significantly different from the region of origin, a new situation results, because the population is free of competitors or benefits from living conditions not present in the region of origin.

In principle, the fewer species (already) inhabit an island, the more possibilities there are for newcomers. The converse is also true. Islands that formed when rising sea levels separated them from the mainland – such as the British Isles, which until about 10,000 years ago were connected with the European continent – therefore have few species that are unique to them (endemic species). In contrast, on remote oceanic islands that rose from the sea millions of years ago due to volcanism, the newcomers quickly develop into autonomous species. This is true on the mainland as well where there is an island-like distribution of certain habitats, for example high mountain summits or lakes that are not connected by rivers. All of this is mentioned here because it is decisive in determining how species survive when their populations become more strongly fragmented. This will be further pursued later.

In summary: the formation of new species is favored by small populations in isolated situations, especially when these situations offer new, completely different living conditions. But this requires time, a lot of time. The process of species formation (disregarding the smallest organisms, in particular viruses and bacteria) typically unfolds over tens of thousands of years and generations. The generation time – that is, the period an organism needs before it is able to reproduce – provides a good approximate value. This gives us a clear rule of thumb: the bigger an organism is and the more time it needs to develop, the ability to reproduce, the slower species formation and evolution occur. Large species are 'genetically sluggish,' as are large populations.

Without change in environmental conditions there would be no evolution. Species would remain stable to the greatest extent. Environmental changes act as a motor which drives the formation of species. Stable habitats preserve the status quo. New life forms arise through change. Equally, it is change that causes species to die out. As with evolution, the relative threat and possible speed of extinction faced by an organism depends on its lifespan and generation time. Large populations of widespread species are much more secure than small, local, and isolated ones. This too will be discussed at greater length further on. First we must look at why, under these basic conditions, the tropics are so much richer in species than the extratropical regions. Does warmth favor the formation of species?

Does Warmth Create Species Richness?

By far the greatest richness of both aquatic and terrestrial species is found in the tropics. Species diversity decreases as the climate cools, both with greater proximity to the poles and with increasing elevation. Warmth would thus seem to promote the formation of species, while cold would seem to inhibit it. It is not the temperature itself that is decisive, however, but how warmth affects ecological processes. Warmth accelerates life processes in general and cold inhibits them (as we know and expect from our refrigerators!). Temperature itself, however, has almost nothing to do with the really important life processes – that is, with growth and reproduction, with activity and processing of information – except when it becomes simply too cold or too hot for certain life processes. Three other main factors have much greater influence on life processes. These are the availability of nutrients or food, energy intake, and water. Water constitutes a universal means of conveyance in nature; in organisms themselves, in their bodies as well as outside them, in the earth, in bodies of water, and in the atmosphere. Water can provide cooling and warming, compensate temperature differences, and significantly influence processes in nature through the formation of water vapor, snow, and ice. In its various forms, water modifies life processes. All higher forms of multicellular, or organismic, life originated in the water. The availability of water places limitations on life possibilities nearly everywhere except in the inner (perpetually humid) tropics and in bodies of water themselves. Where water is available in virtually unlimited supply, life has developed in the greatest variety. Species diversity is promoted under conditions of moderate to scarce availability of nutrients coupled with high energy intake. It is inhibited by abundance of nutrients and scarcity of energy.

A large part of the genetic changes (mutations) that occur in nature can be attributed to the effects of radiant energy. Ultraviolet (UV) radiation plays a particularly important role. It is energy-rich enough to trigger mutations without at the same time destroying larger parts of the genome. The outstanding species diversity exhibited, in different ways, both in high mountains and in the tree canopy of tropical forests (Figure 2) is most likely due to high exposure to UV radiation. Organisms that live sheltered from UV radiation in the deep ocean, subterranean caves, or deep in the soil can usually only change through new combinations of existing genes. This makes them 'conservative.' The fact that numerous primeval organisms have existed almost unaltered for millions of years in the deep sea and in dense tropical rainforests has to do with this.

Stability of the environment thus means more than only minimal temperature fluctuations or a very regular annual rhythm of summer and winter. Seen globally, the consequence of this is that in the tropics we find a great number of 'young species,' no more than several hundred thousand years old, as well very primeval 'living fossils.' How fast species change and new species arise depends on whether the mutations to new genetic properties that trigger species formation occur frequently enough and can be maintained for long enough for the combination to be favorable and 'fit.' Warmth alone thus does not result in a rise in species diversity. It is the warmth-related outer conditions of non-living, or abiotic, nature that have made the tropics so rich in species. These conditions are the reason that in extratropical zones, too, the warmer regions have developed so much greater species-richness than the colder ones. Where energy, and above all radiant energy, is abundant, life can flourish and can use the basic resources, up to the point where the moderate scarcity that promotes differentiation into various species comes about. For understandable reasons, this does not work so well on the polar icecaps, since two of the main factors are virtually absent there: the availability of free water and of radiant energy. In the sea, where nutrients are in overabundant supply, polar waters are, from the perspective of us land-dwellers, astonishingly productive despite the cold conditions.

But at sea as well we find the greatest variety in the tropics – in the coral reefs, which fully correspond to terrestrial tropical rainforests as centers of species diversity. This is more difficult for us to grasp, as in the ocean we cannot see the basis of productivity, the dissolved minerals, or the first consumers, the tiny plant plankton, with our own eyes, whereas it is obvious to us that nutrient-rich meadows or dense forests are not deserts. True productivity is measured by the rate – the amount per unit of time – at which organic substances are newly formed. The biomass generated by a temperate forest producing 100 tons of leaf mass per hectare annually along with new wood growth can be much less than that generated in the same period by dozens of reproductive cycles of microscopic algae, organisms that can be seen only due to the pale, greenish tint they give to the water. The turnover resulting from build-up, consumption by other organisms, and breakdown occurs much more quickly in the ocean than in a forest. It is thus no coincidence that the largest animals on the planet, the great whales, thrive in cold, nutrient-rich regions of the sea where they feed on masses of tiny krill. The water bears their many tons of body mass. The productivity of certain areas of the ocean nourishes them so well that some whales only feed for a few months of the year, before migrating to 'nutrient-poor' tropical waters for the winter to bear and deliver their young and mate. The steps of consumption involved are joined in food chains or food webs, depending on how extensively they are interconnected.

These aspects – the supply of energy, for which the external temperature is a fairly good measure, and the availability of nutrients that are used during faster or slower turnover cycles – indeed explain much, though by no means all, of what determines biodiversity. This is because, to put it simply, if a particular species does not exist, it cannot affect the ecology of an area. Polar bears occur around the North Pole but not in the Antarctic, since members of the bear family have not spread far enough into the southern hemisphere to be able to colonize the edge of the Antarctic ice. Conversely, the penguins, whose main populations are concentrated here, are not found in the Arctic. These examples should be sufficient to suggest at this point that it is not alone the living conditions (ecology) that are decisive, but also the natural history of the organisms (evolution) that has led to a highly uneven distribution of species over the continents and oceans.

Species Richness Over Long Periods (Evolution)

Hummingbirds are to be found only in the Americas, kangaroos in Australia, and tree kangaroos in New Guinea. The platypus, one of a handful of egg-laying mammal species in the world, occurs exclusively in Australia. Two very similar species of another semi-aquatic mammal, the beaver, inhabit northern Asia and Europe (European beaver *Castor fiber*) and a large part of North America (American beaver *Castor canadensis*), respectively. The osprey (*Pandion haliaetus*) is a 'global citizen' distributed across most of the world, but is rare to extremely rare over its entire range. The English or house sparrow (*Passer domesticus*) has in historic times spread, with Europeans, across Southwestern Asia and Europe, and in the last two centuries over the whole world except for the polar regions. The crested tit (*Parus cristatus*) is among the few exclusively European species in the bird world, while the great tit (*Parus major*), a ubiquitous presence at bird feeders during the winter months, is spread from Southwestern Europe to East Asia, including Japan, and has given rise to numerous and quite easily discernible forms (subspecies) in this enormous range.

This has parallels in the plant world. Some species of eucalyptus trees grow so well in Mediterranean Europe that they have gained precedence over native tree species, even though they come from distant Australia. The melaleuca plant spread out so aggressively in Florida that it provoked concern for indigenous species. Thistles from Europe did the same in the pampas of Argentina, rabbits in Australia, and so forth. The fact that many species live only in particular regions does not mean that they could not live anywhere else. Rather it is usually their evolutionary history that is decisive. Australia was a very isolated island continent for many millions of years. Completely independent developments transpired on this land mass during the Tertiary and the Quaternary (the geological present), that is, during the last 65 million years. South America was similarly isolated, though not for quite such a long period. A land connection was created about three million years ago when a section of the earth's crust in the eastern Pacific, the Nazca Plate, wedged itself between the continental masses of North and South America. This led to volcanic activity (and strong earthquakes, which to this day rock the western coast of the Americas). Island upon island arose, until these eventually were joined together to form the Central American isthmus. Some 70 million years earlier there had been a similar, even larger connection, which was subsequently 'pushed through.' Its remnants now constitute the islands of the Caribbean, including Cuba, Jamaica, Hispaniola, and the Antillean arc.

The new land bridge made possible, over two and a half million years ago, what was likely the greatest exchange of animals and plants in the history of the earth, the Great American Biotic Interchange. Around half of the mammal families now present in South America are of North American origin and are represented by 'modern species' such as deer, cats, and foxes. Curiously, the North American species (North America in the zoogeographical sense, the 'Nearctic' to experts) proved considerably superior to those of South America. As a result, far fewer representatives of this extraordinarily species-rich continent succeeded in advancing northward through Central America. Characteristic South American species, such as sloths, anteaters and armadillos remained largely or completely confined to their original area or advanced only as far as the border regions of the tropics on the North American side. The birds were more successful. Due to the South American influence, the bird world of North America differs from those of Europe and East Asia to a greater extent than is the case for mammals. Thus, well-researched geological processes show both the independence in the long-term development, which for example made Australia the continent of the marsupials (although there are also several marsupial species in South America), and disparities in the ability to compete and spread out that arose from the environment in which the species lived. Low competitive strength puts species at risk of displacement and extinction. In this sense, island species face a much greater threat – as will be explained in more detail below – than mainland species, which from the outset have been exposed to various kinds of competition as well as varying environmental conditions.

The formation of new species takes time – a great deal of time as measured from human's temporal perspective. Even tens of thousands of generations are seldom sufficient to bring forth new species (with the exception of microbes). The development of species, and especially of new phylogenetic lines, is measured in geological time, or millions of years. Anything that occurs within a period of a million years is considered 'rapid evolution.' Our own evolution, our biological development into humans, took some five million years. At least 150,000 years ago, a new human species, *Homo sapiens*, to which all modern humans belong, developed out of the genus *Homo*, which also included several different, now extinct species. The subsequent partial

splitting into human populations that differ in appearance super-
ficially, yet barely represent biological subspecies (mistermed as
'races'), dates only a few tens of thousands of years. Likewise,
nearly all species of larger animals and plants that we know
have evolved in the last hundreds of thousands of years. Only in
few places and under special conditions does the formation of
species occur more rapidly – in isolated lakes, for example, such
as those that formed at the end of the last ice age.

Thus it is clear that the age of habitats and their history must
have played a decisive role in the development of the present composition of species diversity. Indeed, there are many findings that
confirm this. In very 'stable' and thus also geologically quite old
habitats (biotopes), primeval species still exist. Tropical rainforests are one such type of biotope, or, more precisely, biome, since
they contain many different biotopes. As previously discussed,
they are also especially rich in species (see p. 21). This apparent
contradiction is easily resolved when we look more closely at the
history of the tropics and their forests.

Origins Of Species Diversity In Recent Geological History

Fossil discoveries indicate that in the long warm period near
the end of the Tertiary, from 4.5 to 3.5 million years ago, when
southern England had a subtropical climate, global species richness was especially great, perhaps approaching that of the best
(warmest) times of the Tertiary. But some three million years ago
a series of climatic fluctuations began quite suddenly (in terms of
geological time) and have continued up to the geological present,
the Holocene. In the fast succession of hundreds of thousands
of years, the polar ice advanced or became thicker when the
climate cooled, or melted as the climate became warmer. These

fluctuations included the great ice age cycles, the most recent of which – variously known as the Würm, Weichsel, or Wisconsin glaciation – ended around 10,000 years ago, as well as shorter, equally intense cycles of alternation between cold phases and warm periods. One of the most significant effects was an accompanying cyclical variation in the sea level, which has risen above and dropped to more than 100 meters below that of our times. The rise and fall of the sea level led to previously contiguous terrain becoming islands, and, conversely, islands becoming joined to other islands or to the mainland. Additionally, the ice age climate change was expressed in the tropics in the form of highly varying precipitation. During cold periods of little rainfall, the (wet) forests shrank while dry areas expanded. Warm phases brought renewed expansion of the forests. Thus the ice age climate swings also affected tropical and subtropical regions of the large continents, where they repeatedly led to the island-like isolation of populations of species. As already discussed, new species develop rapidly in isolated populations, whereas extensive continuous populations react with only slow or negligible change. The German tropical biologist Jürgen Haffer aptly characterized this process as a 'species pump,' as shrinking areas of tropical forests effectively became islands, reinforcing small existing differences within species and driving the process of species formation. When the forest-islands again expanded and merged with one another, a general exchange of genes between the previously separated forms was no longer possible. Rather, border areas formed, so-called contact zones, which served to divide more than reunite the populations. The next cycle again amplified the differences, and so on.

It is a consequence of this 'Ice Age pump' that today we find such extraordinary species-richness in the tropics, with many, only slightly varying species. These exclude one another in large part, inhabiting adjacent geographical territories like pieces of a mosaic. Species in such a parapatric distribution pattern have to keep a distance from one another because their respective uses of resources are not compatible. These 'young' species which have evolved through the processes described above sometimes share areas with very old species, because these 'living fossils' were not affected by the same geological dynamics.

The especially species-rich areas of the tropics contain both of the basic forms of species diversity: a (very) old one that has remained, and a very young one that arose as a result of the ice age climate dynamic. This is visibly expressed in the zoological-botanical classification system. The old species are isolated, a single one typically comprising a genus, frequently also a family, and in extreme cases even its own order. They are easy to recognize, as they have no close, and thus similar, relatives. Young species belong to one genus, forming a cluster, and are 'difficult' to classify. Whether they should have the status of an independent species or of a subspecies is sometimes disputed. The same basic pattern occurs among most fish which live in lakes that date to the late or post-Ice Age. Old groups such as the sturgeons are unambiguous. They occur for the most part in rivers, because these are almost always much older than lakes that originated after the Ice Age. Young groups such as the trout-related white-fish (coregons) are the subject of research because nearly every lake has its own 'form' (species, subspecies, or population). It must again be emphasized that the development of species is a process that takes time, as questions of the protection of species and of preserving biodiversity do not deal solely with the conservation of that which exists, but also with maintaining further possibilities of evolution and keeping new paths open.

It also follows from these explanations that the regions particularly affected by the Ice Age, such as Northwestern and Central

Europe and a large part of northern and central North America, have experienced very high species dynamics, as the previous stock of species in large areas was wiped out by the advance of the ice. As the ice melted back, recolonization began. Which species were a part of this depended on which ones survived the Ice Age in areas of refuge, and whether, as the climate changed, they were able to spread out again from these areas. One of the two principal refuges in Europe was the Iberian Peninsula in the southwest of the continent, although it is quite small in area and cut off by the high Pyrenees Mountains. The much larger south-eastern refuge stretched from the Balkans into the Middle East. This region provided significantly more species for the recolonization of Central and Northwestern Europe. Europe nonetheless remained species-poor, as there were no refuges on the scale of those in East Asia and North America. Additionally, the Alps and the adjoining series of mountain ranges eastward to the Himalaya are oriented in an east-west direction, making them a strong limiting factor in the exchange between north and south, in contrast to North America, where not only the chief mountain range, the Rockies, but also the Appalachians – both geologically comparable to Europe's high and medium-high mountain ranges – run north-south. The climatic belts thus shifted more easily with the fluctuations of the Ice Age in North America (and, correspondingly, in the southern reaches of South America) and in East Asia than they did in Europe.

In Europe the post-Ice Age development of the forests was in all probability not yet complete when humans began to alter nature, turning natural woodlands first into economic forests and, finally, planted ones (Küster 1998). In the ten thousand years since the end of the Ice Age, Europe could not have achieved a 'stable' animal and plant world, not only due to the continual and considerable changes the climate underwent during this period, but also because a handful of successive tree generations in one forest type would not have been sufficient to bring this about. After all, an oak naturally lives for 500 years or more (unless it falls victim to the axe or saw). Other characteristic forest trees, too, reach a natural age of between 500 and 1,000 years. The discovery of pollen from forest trees (and bushes, such as the hazel *Corylus avellana*) that has survived, well-preserved, in the layers of raised bogs indicate a major post-Ice Age change in the forests. Such a change also took place during earlier interglacial (warm) periods. The abundance of some tree species increased or decreased, briefly achieving a high share for a short time, only to nearly disappear again; or remained at essentially the same low level for centuries. This information allows us to deduce not only which growth conditions predominated in earlier centuries and millennia, using modern-day requirements of the various tree species as a point of reference, but, especially, that there has not been a sustained stable state in nature in Europe in the last centuries and millennia. The appearance of humans as well, who through agriculture and animal husbandry first influenced and then permanently altered the continent's landscapes, can be recognized and followed by means of this natural testimony. And this was the case not only in Europe, but almost everywhere on earth, because at the end of the Ice Age almost the entire world had been populated by humans. The only exception was the perpetual ice at the poles, because humans could venture only as far as the edges of the ice.

However, for many plant and some animal species, our presence has meant that in recent millennia we have become a 'factor of selection.' There are many indicators and a great deal of direct evidence that humans killed off numerous large animals toward the end of and directly after the Ice Age. It is certain that animal and plant breeding has resulted in new forms of life. Crop plants became significant thousands of years ago; the cultivation of land gave rise to new living conditions and, with this, new conditions of selection for animals and plants. It has been determined that numerous plants – in some European areas, just under half of the plant species of the open cultivated land – have come about through hybridization and polyploidy. This finding, too, is an expression of the long duration of human influence.

Time is a 'factor' that, through duration and change of intensities, has a decisive influence on basic processes in nature, even though time itself does not 'do' anything. It passes through seasons, climate cycles, and successions of generations. Collectively, the changes that arise from such processes are what we call evolution. The effects of human activity change the processes and thus have become a – sometimes even dominant – factor in evolution. And to repeat this important point: nature is a matter not only of the momentary state and its changes, that is, of ecology, but especially also about the long-term developments, about (natural) history. At any given time nature forms the stage on which the play of life unfolds. The 'stage' is the 'ecological theater,' the play that unabatingly unfolds is evolution. Stage and actors in this great play of life change across space and over time. Ecology takes in only the present. Its consequences remain incomplete so long as natural history is not taken into account. In the same way, any current state in human populations, nations, and political or social systems is impossible to truly understand without the past, without history. Accordingly, the future of the world's species depends not alone on the present, but also on the past, on its natural history.

The Purpose Of Species Diversity

What good are all these species? Would nature not get along fine with less diversity? Or, more pointedly, do we human beings really need some inconspicuous beetle that lives in very specific conditions in some remote place? Are many species not simply insignificant and dispensable? Would it not be better to eradicate all the pathogens that cause illnesses that afflict or kill people, animals, and plants? The answer to the latter question seems obvious when we slap a mosquito attempting to suck blood from our arm, or when we strive to wipe out malaria, at least to the extent that smallpox has been eradicated. Categorical answers to the question of which species we 'need' and thus should preserve, are highly problematic. Two difficulties inevitably arise:

1. Where do we draw the line between, on the one hand, absolutely 'useless' or 'harmful' life forms and, on the other, species that are 'useful,' 'necessary,' or simply 'beautiful'?
2. Who is to serve as the judge who hands down these verdicts?

The question of benefit and harm is seen very much from the human perspective – usually that of a small number of people, in fact. The great majority is not asked, since it is not perceived as being affected by a given problem. From a different perspective or based on better knowledge, today's assessment can tomorrow prove to be in error. And how much do we truly know at present about the so-called balance of nature and how it is maintained? Independent of economic, aesthetic, and ethical assessments, we can determine a number of facts that will again play a role in our later consideration of and justification for the preservation of species and biological diversity. Clearly, the species of plants and animals are not merely a varied bunch of organisms gathered randomly in one location. Whether in a fairly natural state or one (strongly) altered by humans, nature has 'structure.' Plants that grow in a given location can only do so when the local conditions meet their living requirements. These requirements that 'bind them to the biotope' are not nearly so fixed as conservation and environmental literature sometimes suggests. This is demonstrated by the variety of plants and animals that can be found flourishing on cultivated land and in cities. They often form loose communities in which interdependencies develop. Many plant species are dependent on animals, especially on insects, to carry their pollen from flower to flower. Other species of coexisting animals, plants, and fungi develop very close communities which function so well that the relationship, called a symbiosis, brings benefits for all participants that outweigh those of living in isolation. In short, the virtually incalculable abundance of relationships between organisms proves that communities of species are more than an arbitrarily interchangeable collection of plants, fungi, and animals. Yet they are generally not so fixed in their interrelationships that they cannot accommodate changes or are no longer open to exchange and fluctuations. Accordingly, the term 'ecosystem' was coined to denote the relationships between organisms, the subject of the discipline of ecology.

The term refers to parts of nature (biotopes) in which life forms have interdependent relationships with each other and with their non-living environment. Ecosystems are also viewed as 'higher functional entities of nature,' in a sense as 'super-organisms.' But this comparison creates confusion. An ecological system differs from an organism in three fundamental respects. Living things, organisms, can be distinguished by three decisive characteristics.

- They are separate from the outer world. That is, their body surface serves as a boundary between inside and outside.
- They contain an internal functional control that determines their target state. By preventing the organism from deviating too strongly from the target values, this control protects it against harm and death.
- And they are able to reproduce.

Life is perpetuated by organisms. In this, it keeps itself far 'removed from the balance with the environment' by means of separation from the environment. This is crucial. Excepting for prolonged periods of dormancy, life survives over time by reproduction, through which organisms repeatedly 'renew' themselves. The internal (central) control by the genome makes possible the perpetuation of life as well as reproduction over generations and over time. An organism that can sustain itself but cannot produce offspring will die out.

In contrast, ecosystems transform themselves by means of the exchange of organisms and renewal through their reproduction. From the human standpoint, they can be defined almost arbitrarily, as they neither possess a 'naturally prescribed' state nor exist in fixed form. Due to this openness, they are changeable. Humans take advantage of this and alter nature according to their own needs and purposes. Many other organisms do so, too, or attempt to. Elephants alter broad expanses of forest and bushland. Tropical ants in the Americas engage in underground 'agriculture' in the form of fungus gardens that they 'feed' and fertilize. Trees, growing together in forests and stretching skyward, change the local, regional, and even the global climate. The greatest visible environmental transformations caused by living things are the coral reefs. The Great Barrier Reef off the eastern coast of Australia extends over hundreds of kilometers through the tropical South Pacific.

Figure 1 In over-fertilized Central Europe, flowers are seldom found in their former colorful variety, except in special locations such as on dikes

Figure 2 Mass blooms of dandelion (*Taraxacum officinale*) are evidence of the excessive fertilization of grazing lands

Figure 3 The reintroduction of the beaver (*Castor fiber*) is among the greatest successes of species protection in Central Europe

Figure 4 For centuries, the European bee-eater (*Merops apiaster*), with its tropically hued plumage, has periodically bred north of the Alps

Figure 5 The peppered moth (*Biston betularia*), in its normal gray and variant black ("industrial melanism")

Figure 6 Even the once-common marbled white (*Melanargia galathea*) has become rare

Figure 7 The corn poppy (*Papaver rhoeas*) came to Central Europe as a weed centuries ago

Figure 8 Himalayan balsam (*Impatiens glandulifera*), in and of itself a benign and beautiful flowering plant favored by bumblebees, also has become an invasive species

Figure 9 The giant hogweed (*Heracleum mantegazzianum*) benefits from over-fertilizing, which has made it into an invasive species

Figure 10 The American bison (*Bison bison*), or 'buffalo', only narrowly escaped extinction

Figure 11 Goats on one of the Galapagos Islands have eaten all of the vegetation their muzzles can reach

Figure 12 The marine iguana (*Amblyrhynchus cristatus*) of Galapagos looks like a relic of a primeval animal world

Figure 13 Animals in the Galapagos Islands, such as this large male sea lion (*Zalophus californianus wollenbaeki*), are not at all shy of humans

Figure 14 It is not the photographers but a flying fellow member of its species that interests this Galapagos buzzard (*Buteo galapagoensis*)

Figure 15 In the great national parks of East Africa, the lion (*Panthera leo*) can be sized up at close range without danger

Figure 16 A true endemite, the Seychelles (or giant) coconut (*Lodoicea maldivica*) grows only on the Seychelles island of Praslin

Figure 17 The captivating white tern (*Gygis alba*), seemingly familiar with humans, at its breeding grounds in the Seychelles

Figure 18 The sooty tern (*Sterna fuscata*) breeds on remote tropical islands in colonies numbering in the millions

Figure 19 A tropical forest burns in South America

Figure 20 Several million hectares of tropical forests of high biodiversity are destroyed each year in South America to produce feed for livestock in Europe

Figure 21 India is home to around 180 million sacred cows, which produce large quantities of the greenhouse gas methane

Figure 22 In South America, where a tropical rainforest rich in life once stood, gaunt zebu cattle now graze

Figure 23 A Central European mountain spruce forest in a near-natural state

Figure 24 Spruce monoculture with very low biodiversity

Figure 25 The Northern Bald Ibis (*Geronticus eremit a*) is
extremely endangered. Captive breeding programs
are in place to save it and release specimens back into
the wild

Even more significant, however, was the 'invention' of photosynthesis by blue-green bacteria several billion years ago. Like green plants, which are based on them, the metabolism of these simple organisms produces oxygen. It was blue-green bacteria that, through this process, were responsible for supplying oxygen as a gas into the earth's atmosphere. Oxygen in turn created the basis for the development of land animals and for activity requiring consumption of large amounts of energy. In this way, from an ancient waste product of simple organisms arose the decisive condition for the development of higher life forms, including the ascent of humans.

For a good two centuries, humans have been drawing coal, petroleum, and natural gas from the transformed remnants of millions of years' worth of the earth's surplus plant production. These 'fossil fuels' have powered the technical and economic advances of the industrial age. Equilibrium between organisms and their environment has been struck, at best, regionally and, in terms of geological time, temporarily. The driving forces of new developments, of further evolutionary steps, have always been set in motion by change. This at once fundamental and grand build-up and shifting of ever new imbalances has also, since the beginning of life on the planet, brought with it huge problems. Transitions from one state to another do not take place 'harmoniously' or in a manner 'agreeable' to all parties. Nature does not have fixed 'target values' that are necessary to ensure that life processes transpire optimally. The existence of such a state would have precluded evolution. At best, there would only have been the possibility of fine tuning, which would have excluded greater changes and progress.

Based on all that we know, the ability to recognize 'good systems' and work to preserve them is unique to human beings. Our responsibility for our dealings with nature grows out of this awareness. Nature is too multifaceted for such responsibility to be derived from assumed or merely desired 'purposes' of the workings of nature. Almost as in a game of chance, this multitude of possibilities prevents the setting of calculable limits or boundaries. And even if we could capture nature in a single notion, as the sum of all inanimate conditions and all living things, this would not produce a 'person' that we could stand apart from. We ourselves belong to nature. We come from the earth. We did not stop over on a journey from some distant, undiscovered planet. The earth is thus our earth, the only one that we and all living things have available to us, now and in the future. For this reason, the question of 'the purpose' of any other species is too facile, as well as simply falsely posed. In the following chapter we will examine more closely how organisms live. We will see that there is a startling (though actually very natural) accordance between this and the life of humans. Our population development can be described similarly to that of animals. This holds as well for the problems of how we use the environment. It should be no surprise, then, that many of the technical terms that we apply to people correspond to those of general ecology.

3 Living Diversity

Living In Populations

All living creatures need to live with members of the same species if they are to survive. This is not quite true for microbes, but this discussion is not about them. For animals as well as plants, an individual life may last ever so long, but at some point, it comes to an end. If a creature has not reproduced, its individual death also means the end of the lineage it represents. However, the extinction of species begins even before the last individual has died. It is important to know the critical minimum number of individuals for continued survival of the species as a whole. A few dozen may be enough for it to revive, but a few hundred could be too few if the different members of the species live too far apart. In the final analysis, what matters is the numerical outcome from generation to generation. If it is negative, the population will continue to decline, even if offspring is still produced. Population dynamics, a branch of ecology, describes the basic mechanisms relevant here. It examines what makes populations grow, decline, or die out, what causes oscillations in numbers and how populations deal with them. It is mostly about birth and death rates. If we disregard plants and 'plant-like animals' such as corals, which multiply also by means of so-called vegetative growth (budding, division) as well as those microbes which reproduce by simple

division, then the processes for animals and many plants correspond basically to those for humans.

There are generations and successions of generations. The
stock, the population, increases because of new offspring, but
there are also losses due to deaths. In terms of years or generations as appropriate periods of time, the birth rate makes a positive contribution to developing the population, while the death
rate has a diminishing effect on it in the same period of time.
As long as the birth rate exceeds the death rate on average, the
population will grow. Conversely, it will drop if the death rate
is larger. This seems so unremarkable that we might consider it
unnecessary to examine it more closely. But our experience with
the interest on savings or with the development of bank accounts
disabuse us of this notion, for we don't easily grasp such processes by intuition. We tend to think of developments as linear
even if they are actually exponential. People who take out a long-
term mortgage and pay it off in small installments have to pay
quite a lot for interest, sometimes even substantially more than
for the original amount of capital. For even small growth rates of
a few percent, indeed of just a few tenths of one percent, imply
increasingly fast growth of the stock or the costs, regardless
whether we are talking about a population or about capital. This
type of increase is called 'exponential growth' and is differentiated from simple increases, 'linear growth.' The latter is easy for
us to understand. It develops, as does time, in a regular pattern
without increasing the speed of change. Not so for exponential
growth. Even simple series make us stumble after just a few steps
(and have us reach for a pocket calculator for help): 2, 4, 16,
256, 65, 536, and so on, and rapidly to infinity. Mere doublings,
as they occur when bacteria multiply, for example, are usually
underestimated as well. If a germ (which has become resistant to
an antibiotic) divides in two just twenty times, the resulting total

number will range in the millions, and will continue to develop rapidly to very large numbers: 2, 4, 8, 16, 32, 64, 128, 256, 512, 1,024, 2,048, ... 1,048,576. If it divides every twenty minutes, then it takes less than seven hours for it to reach this number (and for the affected organism to get sick). If all the eggs laid by a population of one hundred breeding pairs of blackbirds per year (in two broods with five eggs each) were successful and yielded juvenile blackbirds that survived to the next year and then multiplied in the same way, the number of blackbirds would jump to six thousand in just two years – sixty-fold the original number. The increase would be even more extreme for insects or plants that generate millions of seeds per generation. It is obvious that appropriate mechanisms opposing these developments must take effect, otherwise a small handful of species would flood the entire planet in a short period of time and would make it uninhabitable for all other life forms.

Our own world population, the population of the species *Homo sapiens*, has been increasing exponentially since the nineteenth century (see *Overcrowded World* by R. Münz & A. F. Reiterer in this series). This type of increase is characteristic of life forms in general, by no means only of humans. Every animal, plant, fungus, and microbe species would experience such exponential growth in the absence of very effective 'brakes.' These adversaries are part of the living and physical environment. Taken together, they are called environmental resistance against growth. Their effect is that after the population has increased sharply at first, growth weakens and finally ceases entirely, or that the result is more or less regular oscillations, a fluctuation of the size of the population.

Examples for this include colonies of bacteria under controlled laboratory conditions, in which growth takes place almost as in the numerical series above, and the populations of mice in the wild. The development of most species, however, follows an s-shaped (sigmoid) growth curve. It can be divided into three sections that are easy to discern. It takes a while at the beginning for population growth to gather momentum. This section is called the lag phase. The longer it takes for the animals or plants in question to reach sexual maturity, the longer this phase. Elephants take much longer than mice, humans much longer than mosquitoes. This is one reason for the lag phase; another is the initial lack of suitable partners for reproduction, so that population growth does not really gain momentum immediately. That changes as the population continues to grow. Once enough individuals are present, the phase of strong growth begins, the 'exponential phase.' Humankind currently seems to be at the end of this phase. A decrease of growth can be observed when it changes direction discernibly and takes course towards attaining a final population level that can be estimated in advance. Species that respond well to the environment's carrying capacity, or environmental capacity, reach this 'stationary phase' without major fluctuations of the population. They do not shoot beyond the environmental capacity. They regulate their own population growth in time.

But such species are in the minority. A great many of them do not respond to the environmental limits early enough. Population growth continues at too high a rate and is slowed too late. The consequence is that the population, which has grown too big, exceeds the carrying capacity of the environment, and that the environment is overused. It now follows inevitably that the population will shrink rapidly, which in the extreme can result in its collapse. It then takes a while again for the population to recover and for population growth to begin anew, which in turn will follow a similar course. Species of this type display very strong oscillations in their numbers, all the more if the environmental conditions they are subjected to fluctuate sharply, due to weather conditions, for example. In contrast to the previous type, whose species are able to adjust their rate of reproduction to the environmental capacities still available and limit their offspring to the 'slots' which have opened up due to deaths, the highly fluctuating species disturb or destroy their environments again and again, at different times and in different places. Only in the long term and after many periods of strong growth and decline do they adjust to their environment's capacity, a stage which is attained more directly by those species that regulate their reproduction better. The fact that there is so much change and dynamism in nature is therefore by no means a result solely of the inanimate forces such as weather and climate, availability of water, and other factors, but is also due to the living creatures themselves. They are both part of the dynamism and its driving force. And at times, they engender the risk of dying out on the spot because their populations have attained self-destructive dimensions. In fact, this occurs very frequently. The fact that the species do not die out immediately is due to an entirely different part of population dynamics which we humans, too, are familiar with from our own experience, but which we want to control at a low level or rule out entirely: immigration and emigration. They reinforce the development resulting from the birth and death rates, or they weaken it, depending on the phase of development and the extent to which immigration or emigration takes effect.

For example, immigration from another population of the species, that is by individuals from an incidence nearby, can shorten the initial lag phase because it augments the offspring produced by the local population itself. The founding of a new population often springs from such immigrants. If immigration continues, the phase of strong growth is intensified further, and the limits of environmental capacity are reached more quickly.

But usually, emigration begins even while the population is still growing. Initial losses due to emigration delay this development. Reintroduction projects above all must cope with these losses, because in principle, they weaken the new population just as deaths do. But increasing numbers of members of the population emigrate when it has grown substantially and is approaching the limits of capacity. These emigrants can then found new populations elsewhere.

The actual rate of change that occurs in a population is therefore the result of four processes: birth and death rates, immigration and emigration rates. Births and immigration support population growth, deaths and emigration reduce the population's size. Both immigration and emigration connect a particular population with its surroundings, with parts or all of the species, depending on how dispersed it is. They embody the geographical side of population dynamics. This aspect is often neglected. As we will show below, fragmentation of a species in several or many populations is of utmost importance for its survival, because local losses or even disappearance in one place can be compensated by productive populations in others.

Provided they exist! The term meta-population is used for this phenomenon; in ecology, it means that the individual populations of species are networked via immigration and emigration. If this interconnection works because the populations of a species are actually in contact with one another, it helps secure the survival of the species to a much greater degree than the local conditions, as favorable as they may be. For limited populations also reflect distinct local characteristics of the environment which have selective effects, thereby curtailing genetic diversity. Although local populations are more quickly able to change and undergo evolutionary processes than large, contiguous ones, they are also affected by a heightened risk of extinction. The more isolated a population is, and the more homogeneous in genetic terms, the easier it is for specific germs to spread and to annihilate the population in a particular place. Even minimal environmental changes can exceed the local population's ability to handle the situation because it does not have enough options for adaptation.

Again, human beings experience many similar cases. For instance, numerous (small) indigenous groups ('tribes') in South America died out when 'simple diseases' from Europe, such as measles, smallpox, and tuberculosis were introduced to their previously so isolated areas. Their population size was too small to be able to sustain and compensate the sudden losses due to these diseases. Conversely, European settlers who had moved to South America in small, very closed, and well-organized groups, for example to Gran Chaco in Paraguay, succeeded in developing highly prosperous, growing colonies in just one or two generations because they were skilled at using the resources available there very effectively. Even though they were largely isolated, they still kept much of what defined their cultural and religious distinctiveness. The development was completely different in the large areas where the most diverse populations mixed, melting pots such as the US or Brazil, where many millions melded to form new peoples and take on a new identity after a few generations.

At present, several European countries need immigration, for various reasons, but desire to permit it only in a highly controlled fashion, while from a global perspective, population growth is still strong, even if we do seem to have surmounted the phase of highest growth. These comparisons are appropriate if for no other reason than that they show us, using the example of ourselves, humans, what is very common in the rest of nature. A species can be broken down into local populations which may display different behaviors regarding their reproduction. In addition, the methods of population science as applied to human beings, including their practical application in actuarial statistics, can be used to analyze and forecast developments in the animal kingdom. There is hardly a field in which aspects relating to mankind fit developments for species living in the wild as well as in population science. Conversely, findings gained from experiments with animals can be used for illuminating comparisons with human beings. Many an opinion then turns out to be a stereotype. For example, high density, as in colonies of marine birds, does not automatically mean high stress, and should not necessarily be compared with social problems in big cities. Low density does not increase the rate of reproduction of its own accord, either. Taking a closer look at the mechanisms leading to population growth approximating environmental capacity shows how problematic it can be if we uncritically select 'nature' as our model. Most species attain stability that achieves a balance with the environment by massively curtailing reproduction. Then, only a few privileged members of the population are 'permitted' to reproduce, by no means everyone. Such a system may work, but it is not a viable option for human beings which could be reconciled with our humanity.

Living in Geographical Space

A prerequisite for species being segmented as local populations is the availability of appropriate areas or geographical spaces. A species of bird that lives on a small island much too far away from the next one to make flying back and forth an option for connecting two (or more) populations with one another has no alternative but to survive in just one population. Otherwise, it will die out. For this reason alone, island populations of birds and other living creatures are counted among the particularly endangered species prone to extinction. The same applies to very isolated habitats on the continents. In particular, they include summit regions, mountain ranges, or individual mountains, special habitats such as raised bogs and springs, as well as islands of woods in cultivated land. In between them are the expanses of extensive habitats within which the spreading of species is not hindered much by barriers or insurmountable biotopes of other types. For this reason, the different species should be as prevalent on the continents as would correspond to their particular requirements for living. If this were the case, flora and fauna would be much more uniform. Also, foreign species would not have been able to settle so easily in areas where they do not occur naturally. In addition, there would be no significant difference in the composition of species within a given climatic zone.

But that is not the case. Living nature is more diverse than the living conditions. What is more surprising: the number of species increases with the size of the available area, and even in a way that can be predicted with virtually mathematical precision. This is easy to comprehend when it relates to small areas. Every species requires space to live and survive. In the previous section, we explained why a large number of local populations, the meta-populations, provide the best safeguard against extinction. But why should the number of species continue to increase if the land area exceeds a given minimum, however it may be defined? That could happen at best if new biotopes were to be added which had not been found in that area before! Of course, this assumption holds, too, but it falls far short of explaining why the number of species grows along with the increase in space. In fact, the relationships between the number of species and the land area are so clear that one can even use them to evaluate the species richness of a particular area.

For example, in Central Europe, we can expect about 43 species of birds per square kilometer, 81 on one hundred km2 and 113 species on one thousand km2. This refers to bird species that breed in these areas, in other words, that reproduce here, and do not merely pass through. For any given size of the area between ten hectares and one million square kilometers, we can calculate the expected average number of species. Then, we can compare the actual numbers of species found on the ground with the calculated figures. If the actual number is higher than the calculated figure, the area is (especially) species-rich. If it is significantly lower, then it is impoverished in species. Major cities such as Munich and Berlin have 20 to 25 percent more species of breeding birds than the expected value for their land areas. On the other hand, large-scale agricultural regions cleared out of other habitats for miles around display deficits of up to 80 percent. Many studies from recent decades have shown that this dependence of species richness on geographical size is a general natural principle that holds for all groups of plants and animals which have been analyzed regarding this question.

This research has also demonstrated that on islands, species richness grows more quickly with geographical size than on the mainland, and that minimum sizes are required for a representative fraction of the entire spectrum of species to exist. For Central European birds, this minimum size is between one and ten square kilometers. Even small woods are large enough to host the typical forest birds here. The situation is even better for butterflies and other insects that survive in local habitats of this size, even in smaller ones. Large mammals, on the other hand, need correspondingly larger spaces stretching to thousands of square kilometers if populations large enough for survival are to be secured there. That species richness increases with geographical size expresses one side of the correlation. If we view it from the other side, it becomes clear why this relationship is so important. After all, when geographical size is reduced because semi-natural habitats are converted to other land uses, species richness declines accordingly. When the threshold of critical minimum size is reached, a steep drop in numbers begins which occurs more quickly than would otherwise correspond to the diminishing geographical space. Loss of space is the foremost problem for preserving biodiversity, both at the global and the regional levels. For this reason, minimum sizes of habitats are indispensable for preserving species. They deserve closer examination. After all, it is not easy to understand why this is so. Effects of different species' demands for space and their opportunities and abilities to spread are overlaid with their competition with each other and the large or small size of local populations. In addition, survival can also depend on the limiting effects of other species, in other words, competition. In this area, too, there are similarities with humans and their economic activities, a realm in which competition plays a major role, as is well known.

Living with Competition

The diversity we find in nature does not only mean that there are many species and that they can live in a particular place, but also that they get along with one another if they live in the same area. This is not self-evident, because numerous species use the same resources. Even space itself is one such resource. A second tree cannot grow in the very same location where a tree is already standing. In addition to the tree's immediate location, the roots grasp the ground and extract mineral nutrients and water from it. At the treetop, the primary issue is light, but also nutrients brought by the wind and rain. Even if there certainly are differences in the ways and intensity in which plants use such resources, in the end, they all do need the same minerals as well as water and air. In a given place, they inevitably compete for these resources, and the more similar the needs of the species involved are, the stronger the competition.

The strongest competition, however, stems from the members of a tree's own species in dense stands. Where young growth begins with tens of thousands of saplings on a few square meters, one tree remains in the end: the tree that prevails. This type of competition is called intraspecific competition, competition within a species. Different species compete with each other basically in the same way. In this case, competition is interspecific: competition between different species. The different species crowd each other out. The strongest prevail. If the goal is to harvest a certain composition of species of trees from a forest decades after planting it, then appropriate thinning measures are carried out in the attempt to force this competition. For decades, plant protection products in agriculture i.e. agrochemicals have been suppressing undesired competition for the grain and other crops. In the past, weeds had to be removed by hand or machine to achieve better yields.

The fact that plants are bound to a particular location makes it easy to recognize the effects of competition. It is not as obvious in animals, because most species evade each other, thereby seemingly lessening the pressure of competition. But usually, the opposite is the case. If a plant which is actually weak in competition has attained a particular location early enough, that is, before the stronger competing plants arrive, be it by coincidence or because of favorable conditions, it will be able to prevail because it has gained an edge. The stronger animal, in contrast, crowds the weaker one out and chases it away. As always in nature, there are no clear boundaries. But as a rule, two basic types of competition can be discerned. The first type refers to the kind of competition we usually mean when we speak of it in the context of the business world, namely the stronger muscling out the weaker. The second type is more common in nature. It occurs when the competing species move at different speeds. It is often the case that the smaller and weaker species can successfully crowd out the larger and stronger one by taking away too much of the resources needed for survival. After all, speed, which implies turnover, is often particularly important if an animal wants to use resources. We consider small mice that live off of our grain to be dangerous competition. The basic rule is: the smaller, the faster, and therefore the riskier. Nimble little creatures can finish off sluggish big ones! In this vein, small ducks and coots are vastly superior to swans weighing more than ten times as much when it comes to using aquatic plants in the autumn and winter, even if they would not stand a chance in a direct scuffle with the larger animals. But they do use the aquatic plants more quickly, and their efficiency determines how many swans will survive the next winter to a greater degree than the total amount of available plants does. If the swans were to try and chase the smaller competing birds away, they would no longer have enough time to feed. So it is not surprising that more of the large swans than the small ducks die of malnourishment after long, cold winters. The large animals, however, have a different advantage in the competition. Potentially, they can survive longer because their bodies store more reserves. In nature, absolute superiority is practically non-existent. It is always relative to other species in the particular competition. If the parameters of competition are different, and if it takes place in a different location, its results can be entirely different than 'usual.' We will return to this when discussing the problem of islands far from the mainland, because island faunas and floras are especially susceptible to changes in the competitive relationships. Where competition is strong and persistent, the species which are seasoned fighters for survival have a home field advantage, so to speak.

In sum, the existence of competition means that an individual species cannot develop its actual skills to the full under reasonably natural conditions. Its 'ecological niche' is limited by competition. The ecological niche is the totality of all living conditions that a species needs to survive successfully. Ecologists also call it a species' 'profession' because the activities of life specific to a particular species are expressed in it. At least the species' essential needs for survival must be satisfied in the ecological niche. Behavior and learning as well as the pressure from competition determine the type and extent of its use. For this reason, the existence of other species practically always limits the ecological niche of a particular species. But just as a person's 'profession' is not determined inescapably, but is a field of activity in a community that has to be handled with more or less flexibility, neither does the ecological niche mean a little corner somewhere in nature where the species in question belongs.

Only because some resources are indispensable for individual species can those species be found only in particular places – at least in undisturbed nature. These places where species live are well known as biotopes. They have been called the 'addresses' of species, analogous to ecological niches. Thus, a type of profession can exist at numerous addresses, and many species will live together and side by side because they practice different professions. These simple concepts, in which we intentionally use expressions familiar from the world of human beings, also encompass the dynamics of nature. For professions and addresses change; new conditions open up new opportunities. Cooperation is one possibility, tough competition another. Living nature is at least as lively and flexible as the world of human beings

– possibly even quintessentially more dynamic, because nature's motives are not goals and beliefs, but unmitigated, immediate realities and necessities.

Viewing things in this way, a further correspondence to the world of human beings is inescapable: where diversity is great, many species or different professions/specialists have come to terms with the situation. They get along. Where a few species dominate, diversity can (no longer) be sustained or developed. But how do the species manage to live in the same space at the same time on the same resources? The basic principle is to minimize competition or largely avoid it by means of specialization. Whoever is the best specialist in a particular field may be able to prevail against the competition. For this reason, species-rich habitats usually feature a correspondingly large number of highly specialized species – and vice versa. Specialization develops as a result of competition. Again, island species, which develop with little or no competition due to their isolated location, demonstrate the importance of the interaction stemming from this principle. They frequently turn out to be hopelessly weak in competing with other species that arrive on the island from the species-rich mainland.

However, the higher the degree of specialization, the greater the dependence on the very specific natural resources, and the larger the risk of extinction. For this reason, the prospects for long-term survival are just as poor for absolute specialists as for absolute generalists that can do many things fairly well but have no particular skills. That is why natural selection has usually forced compromises. Practically every species has strengths, but also weaknesses. That keeps them flexible, but occasionally also makes them unpredictable to a considerable degree. After all, if we do not know what traits and abilities lurk in a species, we cannot make useful predictions about its future behavior.

Doubtless, before people began breeding domestic dogs, nobody would have been able to imagine all the diversity we have been able to tease out of wolves, a single species. Genetic diversity therefore also means ecological diversity. Species with flexible genetic makeup are adaptable. The immense number of organisms that human beings have classified as pests expresses these hidden abilities. After all, they have become 'pests' only in the world of humans. They have not been pests since the beginning of their existence.

Let us sum up this section briefly: The often-used term 'ecological niche' (usually not chosen deliberately) is founded on the competition of species with each other. Without it, we would need only the 'addresses,' the biotopes or habitats with the incidences of the species in question, in order to identify them. But in reality, a structure of species emerges, as complex as it is flexible, which does not permit its condition to be determined precisely. The communities of species are simultaneously structured and open. 'Nature' does not tell us what they should be like. Whether they should be one way or another reflects nothing but our value judgments of them. Usually, such valuations occur, if at all, only after human activities and interferences have caused massive changes in the natural resources. Only rarely is there something akin to a natural state we can use as a benchmark in order to assess the changes we bring about. Practically all of Europe and gigantic areas of Asia and Africa have been altered by mankind for millennia. A small number of areas in the tropical jungles, the polar ice deserts, and remote ocean islands remained in their natural state until very recently. Nature that is truly 'untouched by human hands' does not exist. For this reason, there is no way around valuing the state of nature and the entire earth according to man-made standards. That may not make it easier to value nature, but it creates room to maneuver when we make value judgments, so that we can keep up with the times and take local and regional conditions and developments into account. Our valuations need not be dogmatic, but can be developed further in a reasonable manner. If living creatures in total had ever oriented themselves towards a fixed state, life would have died out long ago. After all, using a geological time frame, dying and dying out are the normal state of affairs. We must look into this before we can analyze and evaluate the current situation.

4 Dying And Dying Out

Death Carries Life Forward

In the history of living creatures, extinction is the rule. The overwhelming majority of species that have ever lived, more than 95%, died out after a shorter or longer period of existence. Evidence of their lives is to be found in the form of fossils in the deposits of the various geological times. We must assume that the fossils represent only fragments, as the conditions for fossilization existed only in special circumstances. Nonetheless, the fossils show clear sequences. The oldest layers of deposits contain the simplest life forms. Then, more complex ones are to be found, and over time, the fossils become ever more similar to the species alive today. Some life forms no longer exist. They are to be found only in old layers. Viewed chronologically, the fossils strongly suggest that time and again, from the simplest beginnings, life has continued to develop further. When we organize them consecutively from bottom to top, the genealogical tree of life emerges. From the top, that is, from the present day, down, the most diverse traces and branches of life lead back to a single root, to the origin.

Fossils are one of evolutionary biology's three main sources of evidence. The two others are the differences as well as the similarities in the inner structure and functions of current-day organisms, that is, comparative biology, and modern molecular genetics as the newest technique for approaching the past. It has made it possible for us to verify direct kinship on the basis of genetic makeup. Kinship relations show up in the extent of genetic identity of the organisms compared to each other or also from the amount of divergence from one another. The difference corresponds more or less to the time that has passed between the splitting of one species into two other, following species or phylogenetic lines. A constant process of evolution could be deduced from this. But the sequence of fossils expresses something else. There has not been a simple progression of evolution over time. The more or less distant predecessors of today's organisms did not simply exist ten, one hundred or 300 million years ago. Neither were they in existence for about the same length of time. Almost without exception, the chronological charts of geological history and the history of living organisms (paleontology) do not report round numbers.

For example, the so-called Mesozoic Era ended with the Cretaceous period, the great day of the dinosaurs, roughly 66 million years ago. There was a time during the following Tertiary, the main period of the Cenozoic, during which mammals developed particularly well. This period is called the Eocene and lasted from 58 to 37 million years before the present. The last two periods of the Tertiary were the Miocene and the Pliocene. The former began 24 million years ago and ended slightly more than 5 million years ago. The latter lasted from then until the beginning of the Ice Age, the Pleistocene, which began 1.8 million years ago and ended eleven thousand years ago and forms the fourth geologic era, the Quaternary, together with the present age. Geology breaks these periods down in much more detail. They are similar to the course of human history with all the dates that are so difficult to remember.

The fact that our human history does not stick to 'round

numbers' is easy to comprehend by looking at the dates when rulers gained and lost power, founding dates of empires, wars, and similar events of 'historical importance.' Who would venture to assume that the calendar determined at one point in time would fit all special events brought about by mankind? But why does prehistory not go back into the past smoothly, to the beginnings of life and the origins of the Earth? Time itself surely does not move in fits and starts! The irregularities stem from the organisms themselves, just as in human history, where they were triggered by people.

The similarity is not coincidental. The explanation results from the history of living creatures. Their evolution, the emergence of new species and great innovations, did not simply proceed continuously with time, but in downright episodes. Many of them, certainly all the great caesuras that can be seen in the sequence of fossils, probably correspond to catastrophic events in Earth's history. These events were gigantic volcanic eruptions and outpourings of lava, strong fluctuations of the sea level and presumably also immense meteorite impacts with the explosive power of tens of thousands of atomic bombs. At least one such 'great event' or several following one another ended the age of the dinosaurs a good 65 million years ago. Birds and mammals used the opportunities arising from the new beginning following the annihilation of many life forms. Both increased their diversity from probably rather meager remaining populations that had survived the catastrophic time and became 'dominant' in the now following Tertiary. Songbirds whose songs and beauty we human beings appreciate emerged; mammals developed even to gigantic forms which by all means could have rivaled large dinosaurs.

Towards the end of the particularly warm periods of the Tertiary, the diversity of life on Earth reached new heights. The

climatic roller coaster of the Ice Age, on the other hand, resulted
in the extinction of many species that depended on warmth.
Mankind's phylogenetic line also developed from a group of
large primates whose representatives today are known as the
great apes. In the final period of the Tertiary, about 5 million
years ago, our very distant ancestors split off from those relations from which current-day chimpanzees developed. The climatic ups and downs of the Ice Age advanced the emergence of
mankind. But, surely like the overwhelming majority of long-
term developments of organisms, man's emergence by no means
took a straight, linear course 'towards (present) man.' On the
contrary, the evolution of man was linked to the development
of several types of pre- and early hominids. They died out. Our
sister species, too, Neanderthal man *Homo neanderthalensis,* who survived three times as long as today's species *Homo
sapiens,* became extinct.

Another even earlier human species, 'upright man,' (*Homo
erectus*), of whom both Neanderthal man and we human
beings of today are descendents, may well have existed for at
least one and a half million years. We descend from him, to be
specific, probably from one of his African branches. If the link
via evolution and the splitting off of new species did not exist,
no higher life form would have survived geological times. Since
they did survive, however, we as members of the species *Homo
sapiens* carry not only the vast majority of our species' ancestors genes from the genus *Homo* within ourselves, but far more.
98.8 percent of our genetic makeup corresponds to that of the
chimpanzee. The gorilla is a bit more distant to us, with a difference of 1.8 percent, and the orangutan is yet further away,
at 2.4 percent. In the context of extinction, these findings of
modern molecular genetics, applied even when naming species,
illuminate something other than merely kinship. They prove

the unbroken cohesion of all living things across all time, even though the concrete life forms, the species, have become extinct and will continue to die out.

Only very few life forms last for very long periods of time. They are called 'living fossils.' Their survival depends on exceptional stability of the environmental conditions, not, for example, on the fact that they are (or were) so outstandingly well-adapted. After all, changes in living conditions are normal in the long periods of evolution, and stability is the exception. Therefore, extinction and survival do not constitute a basic contradiction. On the contrary, they are the two decisive sides of evolution. Life continues in ever-changing forms, driven by the interaction of species formation and species extinction. Without extinction, available space would have filled up all too quickly, so to speak. There would have been no opportunities for further developments. If the dinosaurs had not become extinct at the end of the Cretaceous period, mammals would not have had any opportunities to develop, and we human beings would not have come into existence. If the land bridge between North and South America and the Gulf Stream had not developed at the end of the Tertiary as a result of volcanic activity and shifting of continental plates, then possibly even today, bipeds erect like human beings, but with brains the size of chimpanzee brains would be running across the African steppes and savannas. And so forth.

Geology and evolution form a sequence of linkages and coincidences, changes and innovations, just as human history does. This kind of link, which becomes apparent only when we look back, but does not permit sufficiently precise predictions, is called 'contingent.' The history of life is a contingent process that we can understand in hindsight, just as we can analyze human history. But the future is and remains open.

From this perspective, one could conclude the debate about

endangering species and species extinction and lay it to rest as an entirely natural, well-nigh necessary process. Indeed, people argue along these lines from time to time. The questions posed initially arise anew in this context. What is the purpose of so many species? Wouldn't a (much) smaller number be enough? Evolution will straighten things out again, create what is necessary and engender the new from that which has survived.

Such a line of argument, however, is based on the wrong timescale. The developments subsumed in the concept of evolution take place in time spans of hundreds of thousands or millions of years, not in decades and centuries. The eradication of species alive today on account of human activity cannot and must not be justified by the inevitability of extinction – just as killing people cannot be justified by pointing to their inevitable death at a later point in time. Species and the time of their existence correspond to the organism and its lifetime. Only if an organism has produced offspring is its death not final. The death of a species, in contrast, is final if the species has become extinct. Thus, extinction in the Earth's history provides no justification at all for eradicating species in our time, but rather shows how prohibitively long it takes for a replacement for the extinct to emerge, and this replacement might be of any kind, usually a very different one. In the case of larger species with complex structures, in other words the overwhelming majority of animals and very many plants, the development of new species take hundreds of thousands of generations. For this reason, it takes tens of thousands to hundred of thousands of years for modest new beginnings to emerge. Therefore, what is annihilated today might possibly be replaced only sometime in the far-distant future – and maybe only because the further developments have not been determined or predefined.

The risk of extinction is probably even the decisive reason for the immense diversity of life forms on our planet. Today, we must assume that microbes, as disease agents, play a central role here. Diversity is 'insurance' for life, and a surplus of offspring is the investment in that insurance. The only premium in return is survival. Precisely for this reason, local and regional extinction of portions of the species, its local populations, is part of the natural dynamic that sustains diversity. And it is from this dynamic, from the ups and downs of the incidences of species, that the special adaptations as well as the small steps of progress emerge in the form of new, advantageous combinations of genes. They secure the future.

Local And Regional Extinction

The Red List of Threatened Species includes a category 'extinct/lost.' It refers to species that could be found in the area in earlier times, but are now no longer in existence ; their local or regional incidences have died out. This does not mean that the species as a whole is extinct. For example, the rock sparrow (*Petronia petronia*) still occurs in the Mediterranean region, but has been extinct north of the Alps for about one hundred years despite being prevalent in the region centuries ago. The better-known European roller (*Coracias garrulus*), much larger and impressive with its colorful plumage, is also still in existence as a species, even though it has given up its previous breeding grounds in central Europe. We could name many more examples, especially in places where distinctly different climate zones overlap, as in central Europe. In these regions, some species spread while others retreat, depending on the weather. This inevitably means that local incidences of species die out or others, whose permanence remains to be seen, are newly established. This dynamic relating to incidence and abundance is especially strong for insects and

other small animals, as well as for many plants that live in a particular place only for one or two years (annuals and biennials, in
contrast to perennial species). Red poppy (*Papaver rhoeas*), so
conspicuous and unmistakable, may blossom in one place one
year and be gone even in the next, only to appear elsewhere. Or if
the peacock butterfly's (*Inachis io*) prickly black caterpillars with
tiny white dots live on the stinging nettles in your garden this
year and pupate successfully so that the butterflies emerge, this
doesn't necessarily mean that there will be peacock butterflies in
the same place next summer, too.

The incidences of stationary organisms with long life spans
are stable: first and foremost trees and the forests they form.
Birds, too, return rather 'reliably.' But in the smaller worlds of
insects, there may be very different conditions from one year
to the next, or over longer periods of time. Their turnover of
species is high. For butterflies, it averages a third of the spectrum
of species. The difference can be up to 60 percent in comparison
with the previous year, if an unfavorable year follows very favorable ones. Such circumstances make it practically impossible to
make predictions. This applies to smaller plants and a time frame
of decades as well. If we observe a specific place, for example
a garden left to take care of itself, a ruderal area, or a clearing
in the woods that permits growth without human interference,
marked changes will take place. The sequence of species was
even given a term of its own: succession. It denotes the more or
less regular progression of species until something akin to a final
state is reached.

But such states – climax phases – are not really stable and
lasting. Often, cycles occur because sections of forest with
a disproportionate number of old trees collapse and progress
into new sequences, or because storms, fires, and other forces
of nature trigger changes. Stability for longer periods of time

comes about only if we consider sufficiently large areas taken together. Then the ups and downs, the arrival and disappearance of species take place within the large habitats and seem to become meaningless. Only seemingly, however, because the dynamic that makes ever-new variations and combinations of genes occur in species and be tested in real life plays out in the small-scale processes of extinction and new invasion.

Only in exceptional cases can we see directly what is happening. For example, when the appearance of the peppered moth (*Biston betularius*), a common species well-known at least to sophisticates of lepidoptera, changed markedly in the nineteenth century, first in British industrial areas, then in other western and central European ones. The normally light gray form of this moth – dappled with lots of small, dark specks – disappeared for the most part. A similar one emerged in its place with a uniform black-gray color. It was merely a mutant that emerged as a color variant, apparently a response to the heavy air pollution. The pollution had killed off the gray-white lichens on the trunks of trees and had blackened them with soot. It was much harder to detect the black peppered moths against this background than the lighter-colored ones – harder, too, for the birds who caught and fed on these butterflies. This textbook example of evolution made obvious how quickly, even within a few decades, altered environmental conditions can take effect. If there had been a uniform, large-scale incidence of the peppered moth, such a rapid response – which was given a name of its own: industrial melanism – would not have been possible. But since widespread and common species occur locally in distinct populations that do not simply mix freely and follow random stochastic processes, selection could take effect so quickly and change the moths' appearance locally and regionally. Specialists in lepidoptera research, many amateurs among them, have demonstrated that the local populations of some species that display variegated patterns and colorings on their wings differ from one another rather clearly. This is the case, for example, for the mountain Apollo (*Parnassius apollo*), whose small populations can (still) be found locally on the Swabian Alb and the Franconian Alb in Germany or in southern Scandinavia, aside from its main populations in the Alps. If such small, isolated populations die out because the natural resources change unfavorably, then specific combinations of genes are lost. In light of the large number of possible combinations, it is fairly improbable that the same ones will emerge elsewhere by chance. As explained above, the small, isolated populations respond quickly. They are the ones from which new developments, and evolution itself, usually spring. But the smaller the population has become, the higher their risk of extinction. This happens so frequently in nature that even specialists are entirely unaware of most cases of local extinction. After all, conversely, new invading species replace the extinct ones, as it were – as long as the species is still present and in a productive state nearby. The core populations must be able to create surpluses that disperse and 'spread' the species. Otherwise, the instances of extinction will prevail. The inevitable result is a shrinking of the area populated by the species and a heightened state of endangerment. Many species have wound up on the Red List of Threatened Species, a nature conservation warning system, not merely because they are rare by nature, but because their habitats are shrinking and the surpluses they produce are too small to replace lost local populations – if they produce any surpluses at all. The loss of abundance has two components which are connected very closely: direct decrease of abundance to an insufficient level, and an absence of immigrants that could offset the losses. For this reason, local extinction that goes beyond normal fluctuations of the kind that can occur from one year to the next, and that cannot be compensated for by species invasion, represents the first level of endangerment. At this point, simple countermeasures can often still have great effects. Later, when a species as a whole has become very rare, it gets more and more difficult to save it from extinction.

However, practically no species can be kept in a steady state in perpetuity. Chance is always part of the game. It reshuffles even what seems to be adapted best under the given circumstances. Strictly speaking, aside from exceptional cases such as clones (the creation of genetically identical offspring), each and every individual features a unique composition of the genetic makeup of the species which, according to the laws of probability, will not recur. That is what our human individuality is founded upon. It is quite rightly a highly-valued good in terms of our human-ity that deserves comprehensive protection. Whoever has experi-enced dogs or cats as pets will assume as a matter of course that they, too, are individuals with unique characters of their own. Genetics shows that this is generally the case in nature – and must be if the genes are reshuffled from one generation to the next. But it is unavoidable that all the individual combinations perish along with their carriers. That means that it is impossible in principle to secure an existing instance of biodiversity in per-petuity because death inevitably annihilates the new which has been brought forth by reproduction. For this reason, desiring to preserve life in all its variety is an unrealistic ideal, an illusion.

In our own world of human beings, reality also confronts us with the fact that individuals die, entire families die out, and that distinctive features disappear with them, while unpredict-able new beings are born and spread, creating new individual beings. The protection of the individual human being does not exclude his or her death, just as formal protection of all individu-als that belong to a protected species does not guarantee survival and reproduction of the special genetic combinations that these individuals carry – regardless whether we are talking about an eagle or a great whale, a chimpanzee or a mountain Apollo. The genetic similarities that hold for all living creatures enable us to conceive of and manage 'protection' on a reasonable, workable basis.

In the context of species conservation, this is particularly noticeable where other creatures ignore the protection decreed by human beings. For example, one cannot make clear to a bird that it is to differentiate between specially protected butterflies on the one hand and those that do not enjoy such protection on the other when it searches for food. Aside from a few specialists, parasites such as ichneumon wasps simply focus on what they can find, in other words, towards abundance. So it is entirely possible that the last local individuals of a protected species are preyed upon and killed by a natural enemy. If we consider the objectives of gamekeeping for hunting, it becomes evident that this is by no means inconsequential theory, but a fairly commonly practiced goal. For instance, the last black grouse should have been protected by bringing down all hawks and other birds of prey, if possible, as well as the foxes in the more immediate and distant environment. For more than a century, controlling various kinds of predators, in other words crows, magpies, and jays, was considered an especial necessity in order to foster game, that is, the 'good species.' Pest control in agriculture and forestry takes a different, but basically comparable, tack. In all these areas, the stated goal is not to exterminate the pests and the enemies of the useful species entirely, which would be impossible for the most part, but to lessen their negative effects on the species to be fostered.

Hunting and pest control both bank on time. If an instance of local or even regional extinction occurs, it will take more or less time for the species to be controlled to immigrate and spread anew. This frequently occurs on a small scale, and it spans intermediary steps all the way to the global fight against diseases whose eradication can be a generally accepted goal. Taking pity on malaria pathogens or the smallpox virus on account of species conservation is not to be expected. Medical considerations, on the other hand, would argue for safekeeping some pathogens so as to have them available in case they do survive outside and cause new outbreaks.

The fact that we have not succeeded in eradicating such germs globally demonstrates how difficult it is to wipe out life forms that are widespread, abundant, and capable of extremely rapid propagation. After all, they have an immense reservoir of potential habitats that they make use of again and again: in human beings, and in numerous other cases also in domestic animals and crop plants. In our discussion about how to preserve species that are threatened by extinction and are to be protected, particular emphasis will be given to the opportunities for living in local populations. But before we deal more precisely with these aspects directed towards the future, it is necessary to draw some preliminary conclusions regarding species extinction. Why does the nature conservation establishment consider it such a threat? Why should the protection of biodiversity be given such prominence that it was placed at the center of political debate at the Earth Summit in Rio in 1992, ranking equally with sustainable development for mankind? What dimension of species losses does current species extinction entail?

Number of animal extinctions from 1780 to 1990

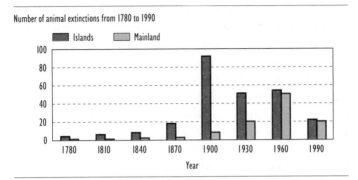

Figure 5   Progress of extinction of animal species between 1780 and
            1990, according to data in Dobson (1997)

On oceanic islands, the losses began earlier than on the continents. In total,
however, the rate of extinction of known animal species is clearly declining and
has dropped almost to zero at the turn of the millennium, that is, in our time

Species Extinction

We do not know precisely enough how many species have died
out in the recent past. Dobson (1997) states that 113 species of
birds and 83 species of mammals have verifiably disappeared
completely since the year 1600. Most of them, more than three-
quarters of the almost two hundred species, lived on (small)
oceanic islands. For the reasons explained above, the species
there are especially endangered even without human interference. Now, if only a good forty species of birds and mammals
died out on the continents in the last four hundred years, which
corresponds to an average of one species per decade, then, argu-
ably, species extinction cannot be considered particularly dramatic. Figure 5 shows the distribution of the documented cases
of species extinction from 1780 to 1990.

However, the number of extinct species would increase

substantially if frogs, lizards, and fish, but above all, insects, snails, and mussels were included. Then, the total number of species that have become extinct in the last four hundred years would be of a magnitude approximating one thousand, which would amount to one ten-thousandth of global diversity, based on a conservative estimate of the total number of existing animals and plants. Even this figure would not contrast enough from the natural rate of extinction taking place 'in the background.' There could be no question of extinction increasing by a factor of a thousand. Also, the natural rate of extinction for insects and other small animals is unknown. This applies to the rate of emergence of new species as well. Oceanic islands form in tens of thousands of years. Well-studied examples are to be found on the volcanic archipelagoes of Hawaii and Galápagos in the Pacific. The age of the individual islands and that of the special animals and plants that developed on them correspond fairly well. Darwin's finches, found on the Galápagos Islands, are even older than the oldest island, and for this reason, they must stem from a stopover before they settled on Galápagos and split into different species. All this happened hundreds of thousands to several million years ago.

Current research was carried out on the island of Surtsey, which emerged from the North Atlantic off Iceland about half a century ago, and especially on the remains of the Indonesian island world after the gargantuan eruption of Krakatoa in 1883. Both were new terrain devoid of life. In the century and a quarter since the eruption of Krakatoa, no new species have emerged, even under the particularly auspicious tropical conditions. This was not to be expected for Surtsey in any case. Speciation, the development of new species, takes time. Practically everyone concerned with preserving biodiversity is convinced that in comparison, extinction can take place quickly, all too quickly, in the world transformed by mankind. Individual, well-documented cases support this hypothesis. For example, half of all bird species on Hawaii have died out in the one thousand five hundred years since people of Polynesian descent settled on this remote group of islands in the North Pacific. No less than twenty-two different species of a very special group of birds called Hawaiian honeycreepers had developed on the Hawaiian islands. In no other place do specimens of this group exist today, nor did they in the past.

Not a single one of the twelve or thirteen species of the ostrich-like moas of New Zealand survived the Maoris' arrival there approximately one thousand years ago. These flightless and probably also tasty birds were easy for the Maoris, who had come from Polynesia, to bag. Likewise, in the seventeenth century, rapid extinction befell the dodo (*Raphus cucullatus*) of Mauritius, a large flightless pigeon living on the ground, when European seafarers reached this previously uninhabited island as well as neighboring Réunion, where the local representative, the solitaire (*Raphus solitarius*), suffered the same fate. 'Dead as the dodo,' as we know, means irreversibly dead: extinct.

Portuguese seafarers had discovered the island of Mauritius in 1507. Around 1680, the dodo had been wiped out. The related Rodrigues Solitaire (*Pezophaps solitaria*) on the neighboring island of Rodrigues lasted about another hundred years, namely until about 1790, and the Réunion Solitaire *Raphus solitarius* existed until 1763. The fates of the extinct are known better and dated more precisely the more recent the final disappearance of a species was. But it was by no means only the island species that were rare by nature which became extinct in centuries past, but also some which occurred in great numbers on continents or islands close to the mainland. The most disturbing example in this regard is the annihilation of the passenger pigeon (*Ectopistes migratorius*) of North America.

Their flocks numbered hundreds of millions of birds. They nested in gigantic, movable, loose colonies in the deciduous forests of what is today the US. To this day, it is difficult to understand how it was possible to completely annihilate a species that was so common – many times more abundant than all our European species of doves and pigeons – in just a few decades. The last specimen of the passenger pigeon died on September 1, 1914, in the Cincinnati Zoo. The last broods in Minnesota had been found in 1885. The reward of one thousand five hundred dollars, announced in the years 1909 to 1911 for locating surviving breeding pairs, was never claimed. Three centuries before, the total population of the passenger pigeon had still been estimated in the billions. And all of a sudden, it was gone. The birds had been shot without restraint, not only for their meat, delicious like that of many pigeons, but often simply as a 'sport.' Originally, the settlers considered the passenger pigeons to be nothing but pests that destroyed their hard-earned harvests of grain when their enormous flocks raided the fields. According to an old calculation, a large flock of passenger pigeons, estimated – perhaps considerably exaggerated – at more than a billion birds, consumed 235,000 tons of grain per day. In light of such horrific numbers, the zeal to annihilate the birds knew no bounds until it was far too late. The much smaller red-billed quelea (*Quelea quelea*), a bit smaller than a sparrow, caused major damage in Africa in the twentieth century, because its flocks, also numbering many millions, came flying in from afar like locusts and annihilated the crops. Pest control on a massive scale has not yet endangered the species.

In North America, planned extermination of the American bison (*Bison bison*) was halted in the nick of time. Leftover populations survived the massacres of the nineteenth century and were resettled and bred in national parks in the US and Canada. Wood Buffalo National Park in Canada is named for the American bison, which returned after its successful rescue from extermination. In the meantime, around one hundred million head of domestic livestock have replaced the estimated sixty million (at their peak) American bison. Rescuing remaining populations from extinction has also succeeded in the case of numerous other species of mammals and birds. The more well-known a species is, the more attention it attracts, the more likely it has become that saving it from extinction can be accomplished.

For this reason, the problem of possible or likely mass extinction refers to the well-known species much less than to the (as yet) unknown diversity of inconspicuous creatures in tropical forests or other natural spaces that are currently being cultivated or simply destroyed at a breathtaking pace. There are very different ways of calculating this hidden rate of extinction (see Figure 5). Since the publication of Dobson's book (1997) a decade ago, experts have been proceeding on the assumption that species extinction amounts to 2 to 3 percent per year. Hence, in the last decade alone, the Earth has lost one-quarter to almost one-third of its species. If this rate were to continue unchecked, and if the basic assumption concerning species loss were accurate, then in 2020, barely half the biodiversity of 1992, the year of the Rio 'Biodiversity Summit', would remain on Earth. Currently, in the spring of 2009, we speak of 150 species dying out per day. The figures given vary by so much that it is almost impossible to find a reproducible point of reference in the confusion. Without a doubt, far and away the most important losses of biodiversity occur in the tropics and subtropics, as they are incomparably more species-rich than non-tropical areas.

It is such considerations and the extrapolations based on them that have given rise to the often-stated fears that species loss of disastrous proportions is taking place almost unnoticed and at a scope comparable to the major catastrophes in geologic times

Species of birds threatened with extinction

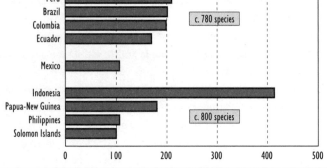

Figure 6   The vast majority of the world's bird species threatened with
           extinction are to be found in two large regions: 780 species of
           birds in the Amazon rain forest and its margins in the Andean
           valleys as well as approximately 800 species in the Southeast
           Asian island world, from Papua-New Guinea and the
           Solomon Islands through Indonesia to the Philippines
           Mexico, which ranks ninth among countries, should be considered part of the
           New World tropics

caused by the impact of gigantic meteorites. Surely, such a worst-
case scenario is grossly exaggerated regarding large animals and
also most plants. But, by definition, what happens in the dark
cannot be observed. We must reckon with the risk of major
species loss as long as enormous amounts of land are deforested,
burned, and turned into plantations in the tropics and subtropics
every year. This affects particularly species-rich areas, after all.
What is lost there cannot be replaced in other places, especially
in the economically rich countries. The geographical distribution
of the species of birds directly threatened by extinction expresses
this very clearly (Figure 6).

In terms of economics and development policy, these countries belong to the group of threshold countries, some of whose economic development is nothing less than tumultuous. So it is not the very poor countries that are destroying their biodiversity out of hardship, but rather the ones that are coming into prosperity and have developed close economic ties to the rich countries. This finding, which holds for numerous other segments of biodiversity as well, must be taken into account in particular when dealing with possibilities for preserving species diversity. Brazil, Indonesia, and other countries do not need to exploit and annihilate their natural resources because of abject poverty. It remains to be seen to what extent we Europeans are indirectly involved in the destruction of tropical species diversity, and are thus responsible for it.

Preservation of biodiversity and sustainable development were not to be mutually exclusive, according to the goals of the Earth Summit of Rio in 1992. Even when different goals overlap partially – one preserving, the other developing – results that reconcile them may be possible. The options are well-known, the means are available, and the goals are realistic. The most highly economically developed countries face the smallest losses of biodiversity, today and in the future. Some prosperous countries, such as Japan, have succeeded in increasing their forests substantially, cleaning up their waters, and protecting far more species than necessary in spite of very high population density. The current return of numerous large animals that had been extinct for a long time in those countries, some for more than two centuries, may be considered the best sign of the fact that much of biological diversity can survive even in very densely populated countries, and in mankind's modern world.

5 Endangering Diversity

Loss of Land Area

Species-richness increases with the size of the land area. This is a central finding of biogeography (which provides a formula for calculation)[*].

On islands of different sizes, species-richness increases with land area even more strongly than it does on the mainland. The general progression of the increase in species with increasing land area can be calculated fairly well. The formula provided in the footnote contains the calculated reference values. However, it requires knowledge of the average number of species of the group in question, for instance, birds, reptiles, or trees per unit of land area (square kilometer, hectare, or square mile). Then, the expected values can be calculated easily and compared with the findings on the ground.

---

[*] $S = C\, A^z$

Number of species (S) = Richness factor (C = average number of species of the group of animals/plants in question per unit of land area, e.g. km²), multiplied by the land area (A, in km² or other units of land area), to the power of z (exponent whose size depends on whether we are dealing with islands or fragmented areas or with a contiguous land area). In the case of contiguous, mainland conditions, z = 0.14; the figure is at least twice as high for island and island-like locations.

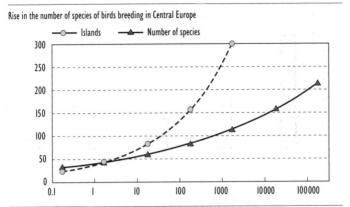

Rise in the number of species of birds breeding in Central Europe

Figure 7   Increase in the number of species (birds breeding in Central
          Europe) as a function of land area (triangles) and the
          calculated progression that would result in the case of island
          conditions (dashed line)

Figure 7 illustrates the relationship using the birds of central
Europe as an example. The numbers of species increase rather
moderately in a manner typical of continental expanses (as
opposed to islands). The value calculated for Bavaria, for
example, is 205 species of birds. That is the exact number identified during the 1996 to 1999 mapping period for the atlas of
breeding birds in Bavaria (Bezzel et al. 2005). Two decades previously, Bavaria was still somewhat below average. The shortfall
has been made up. The expected number of species of breeding
birds in the city of Munich (310 km2) was ninety-six. Yet 110
were identified. In other words, Munich is more species-rich than
areas of the same size on average. We will return to this in the
chapter on the future of diversity. Here, we will first take the
opposite perspective.

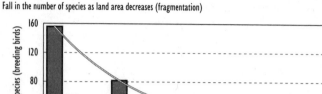

Fall in the number of species as land area decreases (fragmentation)

Figure 8   Marked fall in the number of species (here, breeding birds) capable of survival as the area of their fragmented habitat decreases

After all, Figure 7 also illustrates that decreasing the size of land areas inevitably brings about losses of species. A rule of thumb is that in the case of mainland conditions (i.e., not island conditions), cutting a habitat to one-tenth of its original size entails a loss of at least 50% of its species. But this rule applies only as long as the remaining land areas are still large enough. If they have already been more or less divided into individual bits of land, the loss of species will be much more extensive. This is shown in Figure 8.

Small patches of land cannot sustain the spectrum of species typical for the region. When they have reached a size of about one square kilometer, they are already smaller than the critical size for central European birds. The same holds for plant life, for insects, and also for the fauna in lakes, bogs, and marshes. The next chapter will deal with this question in more depth. However, the number of species that will survive in a larger region depends on more than just the size of the remaining land area available.

As we will show, the distance between the individual areas is a factor as well. For instance, larger birds, especially the water birds with excellent flying skills, can fly distances of up to one hundred kilometers to the nearest bodies of water where their species breeds. In contrast, that is much too far for some small songbirds. For them, even distances of a few hundred meters have an isolating effect.

On an island in a river impoundment listed and well-protected as an international bird sanctuary, for example, it was possible to identify just one-fifth of the species of birds of the river forests that were present at the same time in the large expanse of riparian forest just four hundred meters away. It covered a little more than five square kilometers. The riparian forest on the island, on the other hand, was only a scant hectare in size. In other words, even good protection is insufficient by far to guarantee that the typical birds of the river forests can settle there. The island was simply too small and too far away from the riparian forest on the banks of the river. The situation is similar for a great many protected areas; 2,500 of the protected areas in Germany are smaller than the minimum size of a few square kilometers. That size would be necessary to preserve at least the majority of typical species of small birds and mammals in the protected area. Merely increasing the number of protected areas is of little help if they are not big enough. The further away the nearest protected areas with similar conditions, the larger the individual areas must be. Survival of species in a particular area depends not only on the absolute size of the area, but also on its distance from other areas where they can live. The quality of the biotope itself is often only the third-most important criterion for survival. Even the best area is of no use if it is too small.

Environmentalists have been deploring losses of land area in our central European landscapes for a very long time. "There used to be much more space for plants and animals to live than there is today," is an often-heard complaint. Although that is true, in many cases it is not as important as is assumed. After all, the wealth of species in central Europe has sustained itself surprisingly well over the last hundred years, in spite of all the transformations; in some subsectors, such as birds, species diversity has even increased. For example, a good 20 percent more species of birds reproduce in Bavaria today than at the end of the nineteenth century. The species of birds which were lost have been compensated by more species that have entered the area and settled there permanently. And the really exotic birds, that is, species alien to the area that do not occur in neighboring areas, constitute less than half the increase. This is the case in other parts of Europe as well. Many years' efforts to protect birds have borne fruit. The situation would be similar for insects, plants, and other organisms if the xerothermic, oligotrophic (nutrient-poor) habitats they depend on had not been lost. More on this in the following chapter. Here, we will broaden our perspective from central Europe with its land area of roughly one million square kilometers to the global dimension. After all, the major losses of natural land area are not taking place in this part of the world, but in the tropics and subtropics.

Particularly in South America, inconceivably vast swathes of land are being cleared and transformed into agricultural land that is usually not particularly fertile. In Brazil alone, the amount of tropical forest destroyed per year (!) totals one and a half to three million hectares. In just six years, from 1990 to 1995, 124,000 square kilometers of forest were cleared there, which corresponds to more than a third of Germany's total land surface. However, only a very minor part of this is for poor farmers who clear and settle the land in the Brazilian states of Amazonas, Mato Grasso, or Rondonia. The same is true in other

Destroyed tropical forest 1990–1995 *(in 1000 km² forest/humans per km²)*

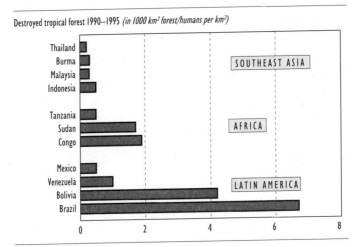

Figure 9   There is no correlation between the size of the destroyed areas
of tropical forests (in 1000 km² forest/human population per
km²) and the human population density in the three major
tropical regions of Southeast Asia, Africa and Latin America

places in the tropics where the forest is annihilated not for the
poor, starving rural population, but for establishing gigantic
tracts of rangeland for cattle as well as plantations that produce
soya or palm oil. Figure 9 shows that there is no statistical correlation between the extent of destruction of the forest and the
population density in the twelve tropical countries most important in this regard. In fact, a statistical correlation does appear
when the cleared areas are graphed against the stocks of cattle
(Figure 10). Two developments of recent decades are taking effect
jointly: firstly, the number of cattle increased sharply in the
course of the last half-century, doubling to approximately 1.5
billion (including the domestic water buffaloes in South East
Asia). As a result, the live weight of domestic cattle exceeds that

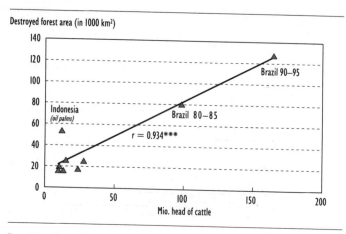

Figure 10   Statistically highly significant correlation between the extent
of tropical forest destruction and the cattle population in the
countries studied
The only outlier is Indonesia, with its oil palm plantations

of all human beings a bit more than two-fold. Secondly, the productive capacity of cattle was increased very sharply, especially
in Europe and North America. Our livestock depends on imports
of large amounts of feed. Soybean meal makes up the major part
of imported feed. Hence, the massive expansion of soy cultivation in the tropics, again, above all in South America, is nourish-
ing the livestock in our barns. Almost literally, our animals are
feeding off tropical forests and tropical biodiversity. The very
large losses of land for natural or semi-natural habitats in recent
times are due to new grazing land for livestock as well as land for
cultivating feed for stabled livestock. What people in the tropics
and subtropics need for themselves and their survival is not only
insignificant regarding the losses of tropical forests, it even disappears into the margin of error of land use data. Indeed, most

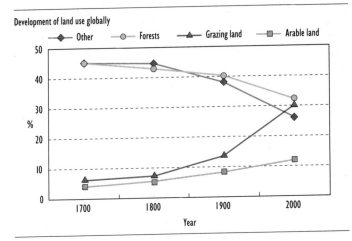

Development of land use globally

Figure 11 Strong increase in grazing land since 1900 compared with
          arable land
          Forests and savannas show the greatest losses

recently, the amount of grazing land increased much more
strongly than the amount of agricultural land for growing crops.
This is shown in Figure 11. But it is precisely these tropical areas
that rank among the most species-rich habitats. So if they are the
places from which feed is exported for the livestock in (central)
European barns, it constitutes a triple burdening of the global
ecological balance. CO_2 equivalents of approximately one thousand tons of forest biomass are emitted into the atmosphere for
every hectare of land burned and cleared without any apprecia-
ble amount of CO_2 being sequestered again later. After all, the
plants in the soy plantations or on the grazing land for livestock
come to only a few thousandths of the previous forest mass. At
two million hectares per year, this results in a loss of biomass
with roughly two billion tons of captured carbon. In addition,

large termites that live on the dry remnants of the plants and emit methane are spreading on grazing land in the tropics in general. Methane is a greenhouse gas, which, in contrast to carbon dioxide, is not metabolized by plants. It is also produced in the rumen and emitted when cattle (ruminants) digest: around two hundred liters per head of cattle per day. Together with the amounts lost in natural gas production and emitted from bogs and swamps, and also from rice paddies, these sources place methane in third place of atmospheric greenhouse gases, following water vapor and carbon dioxide. The third major environmental burden due to animal keeping, after emissions of carbon dioxide and methane, is the immense amount of energy required to produce feed, store it, and transport it halfway around the world until it finally reaches the distant consumers in the barns. At least the plant material grazed on domestic pastures and metabolized into protein, into meat and milk, remains mostly energy-neutral, as do the 'holy cows,' the cattle in India that practically take care of themselves. But these approximately 180 million cattle also produce methane (more than thirteen billion liters per year). If, as shown above, cattle and other stabled livestock already constitute the greatest environmental burden in the world because they consume approximately ten times as much food energy as all of mankind, the climate effects and losses of biodiversity they cause make up additional serious consequences. For it was far less the increase in grain cultivation which occupied species-rich natural areas in the recent past, especially in the second half of the twentieth century, but the considerably larger expansion of keeping livestock (Figure 11). Even in the countries where the poorest of the poor live, for example in large parts of Africa, it is one of the main causes of environmental problems. There, as on some tropical islands, goats as well as cattle destroy the vegetation and turn large swathes of land into wasteland.

Cattle as a status symbol and meat consumption above and beyond a reasonable amount combine to form the major factor for destruction of biodiversity – in this part of the world as well as in the tropics. We have become so accustomed to the overly large stocks of cattle that we do not even perceive how large the numbers are. At fourteen million cattle, twenty-three million pigs, one million sheep, and tens of millions of fowl, the live weight of livestock surpasses that of the eighty-two million people in Germany by far. According to the United Nations Environment Programme, the total land area burned off year after year for keeping livestock is as large as all of Australia, yet this fact has no longer been newsworthy for quite some time. But when, as happens every summer, there are forest fires on a few hundred square kilometers in southern Europe, the media report on this in much detail as if it were a catastrophe. Any sense of proportion has been completely lost here. Following the annual media reports about the summer's fires in the Mediterranean region, a burned area twice the size of Berlin is apparently far more important than burned-off land the size of Australia and the amounts of energy that are emitted into the atmosphere without being used at all. Year after year, these fires in the tropics and subtropics release more energy than Germany uses in total; one-fifth more – or roughly the amount used by Germany, Austria, and Switzerland taken together. Particulalrly during southern winter, that is, summer in the northern hemisphere, when the Earth is viewed from outer space, it looks like a flambéed planet. Since the purpose is to improve grazing land for livestock and obtain more land for cattle and for cultivating feed, this annihilating burning remains unheeded. Only when clouds of smoke drift to Singapore (due to special weather conditions in some years) because the forests on Borneo can be burned off on a large scale do the European media occasionally mention the issue. In the mean time, in this part of the world, the volatile ingredients of slurry escape into the air and make the land stink to the heavens several times a year, without this form of air pollution being taken into consideration. Nitrogen overfertilization has made the substance choke domestic biodiversity. This is expressed by the long Red List of Threatened Species, which grows yet longer with every new study on the ground. The root cause is the agricultural system – in our part of the world as well as in the tropics, where agricultural exports have become the most serious threat by far for tropical biodiversity. These exports and the further development of the conversion of tropical land into grazing land for cattle and soybean fields will determine how much global biodiversity will survive. Given the currently estimated magnitude of forest loss, we must reckon with a loss of half of the Earth's species diversity by the middle of this century. But it is possible that much less of that diversity will remain because the world's appetite for meat is growing, and this development has not shown any sign of tapering off. These effects are magnified in the case of special areas with outstanding biodiversity.

Loss Of Special Habitats

Seen from the perspective of human land use needs, fertile soils are the most productive, especially if they are well-structured and able to store plant nutrients for a sufficient length of time. Loessic and loess-clay soils as well as the humus-rich 'black earth' of former steppe soils in temperate climate zones are best suited for growing grain. In general, this was the reason why steppes and forest steppes above all were taken into agricultural use, as dense grass growth builds up good soils and enriches them with nutrients. Permeable sandy soils are far less suited, and the same is true of soils that are too heavy and wet.

For this reason, one of agriculture's goals has always been to improve the quality of the soil with respect to yields. Wherever possible, wet and damp soils have been drained, nutrient-poor ones fertilized, where deemed proper for economic reasons, and rocks have been removed from soils where they interfered with agricultural use. Melioration stood for improving yields. Long-term use was to be guaranteed by recycling at least part of the nutrients that were removed from the soil by the harvest. Only in a few regions are the soils so good by nature that the erosions caused by intensive use remained insignificant. Such soils could be burdened with long-term intensive use, for example the loess regions in China.

It should be noted as a special case that some river valleys offer similarly favorable conditions because flooding deposits fertile silt time and again. The first major permanent agricultural crops emerged in this kind of river valleys, for example on the lower Nile or on the Euphrates and Tigris. Because of the general relationships between nutrient-richness, productivity, and biodiversity, such highly productive areas were already fairly species-poor by nature. It was relatively easy to convert them to the permanent uses of agriculture and animal husbandry. By definition, agricultural cultivation of land relates to fixed land areas taken under cultivation. Only under special conditions it is possible to practice shifting cultivation, but with low yields. Animal husbandry, on the other hand, took exactly the opposite tack: at first, for centuries or millennia, it was practiced nomadically. The herders roamed the countryside with their herds, imitating the natural behavior of the non-domesticated grazing animals. Permanently keeping animals on limited expanses of land, for example plots in private ownership, is an unnatural innovation.

It rapidly results in overgrazing. Without longer periods during which the grazed lands can recover, much less livestock can be kept on a long-term basis than if the herds are able to roam.

Keeping livestock in enclosures, which implies bringing feed to the animals and removing the waste – droppings or slurry – and dealing with them appropriately, magnifies these problems. Good yields are achieved only if the animals in the barns can be fed high-quality feed. For this reason, keeping livestock in enclosures depends on the additional purchase of feedstuff. If the farm's own land were to supply enough feed, it would usually be more economical, too, to leave the livestock to graze outside as long as possible. The more feed must be provided for the animals kept in enclosures, the larger the amounts of wastes, in the form of droppings or slurry, that must be disposed of. The relationship of the size of the herd on the one hand to the land area on the other is quickly lost.

Cultivation of land, on the other hand, is related to the land surface from the outset. Yields depend on the quality of the land's soil and nutrients as well as on the course of the weather. Yield improvements can be achieved by appropriate fertilization and melioration activities. Irrigation and drainage provide for medium amounts of moisture in the soils, where possible. Drainage in particular has been and continues to be especially important in the yield-rich climate zones with summer rains. For (modern) methods of keeping livestock in enclosures, on the other hand, quality and productivity of the land areas no longer play a role if the farm is mostly run using ready-made feedstuffs. And the business is no longer dependent on the weather, either. Thus, livestock can be produced with hardly a link to the amount of agrarian land. As the animals require high-quality feed, the agricultural land corresponding to raising the livestock is fertilized heavily, and high-performance feed crops are grown. In business terms, this is usually not enough, because for every kilo-gram of meat produced, many times more feed is required, which in turn must be produced on correspondingly large areas. As long as it is cheaper to buy additional feed from elsewhere than to produce it on the farm, the size of the land area for disposing of slurry limits the capacities for keeping livestock enclosed – and not vice versa, as is the case for natural production.

The consequences of this modern form of agricultural pro-duction can be divided into four main effects. The first two parts are the more positive side: (1) structural standardization of the conditions of production (for example, reallocation and consoli-dation of agricultural land holdings) and (2) marked increases of production. On the negative side: (3) the environmental burdens on soils, air, and groundwater, and (4) the losses of biodiversity.

The structural losses were at the beginning of the great agrar-ian transformations of our time. Reallocation and consolidation of agricultural land holdings as well as hydroengineering activi-ties to drain wet areas made the agricultural land more uniform and cleared out everything that could be in the way. Equalizing the conditions of production was (and usually still is) the stated goal. Land to be used for agriculture was to permit the use of machinery to the greatest extent possible – the larger and more uniform the land areas, the better the conditions for employing large machinery. Compared with before, the numbers of con-spicuous structural elements of the landscape such as hedges, thickets, field banks, small damp depressions or escarpments were (very) severely diminished. Newly planted hedges, straight as a die so as to make the least amount of shade on the fields, could not nearly compensate for what had been cleared out by the reallocation and consolidation of agricultural land holdings. These structural changes, which for the most part took place between the 1950s and the 1970s, resulted in losses of visible peripheries and linear boundary markers of up to, and even surpassing, 80%, with some regional differences. Correspondingly, the degree of fragmentation of the remaining habitat areas increased strongly. Small bodies of water in the fields were now too far apart, if they still existed at all after the land holdings were restructured. Frogs, toads, and newts could not migrate between them any more.

Draining wetlands, irrigating arid zones, clearing forests, and overfertilizing coastal wasters are among the main causes of biodiversity loss at the global level as well. After all, they affected those natural spaces in particular that feature high concentrations of biodiversity. The effort to preserve the diversity of life on Earth is not as much about the large, uniform areas as it is about the special habitats. At the global scale, they do not take up much more space than they do at the regional level, to be precise, less than 10% of land in those regions that are suitable for more intensive agricultural use at all. If all of Antarctica, with its 14 million square kilometers, were to be deemed a strict nature reserve, of course, global diversity could not be preserved. The areas which are primarily supposed to serve the preservation of nature must correspond to the actual distribution of biodiversity. Islands, particularly small and remote ones, fall into this special category without further ado.

Geographically, the biodiversity hot spots we must be concerned with first and foremost are to be found in Central America and the western Amazon region, including the tropical valleys of the Andes, in the Atlantic coastal rain forest of Brazil, in the Cape Province of South Africa, in the mountains and (volcanic) plains of east Africa, in the coasts and islands of the Mediterranean region, in the mountain valleys of southwestern and southeastern Asia, in southwestern China and the neighboring areas from Burma to Vietnam, in the island world of the Indo-West

Pacific, especially Indonesia and New Guinea, as well as in areas of northwestern and western Australia. Large portions of Madagascar as well as numerous islands in the Pacific and Indian Oceans are also to be counted among these global priority areas.

Hence, the overlap of the areas important for feeding mankind and for sustainable development on the one hand, and the major regions of biodiversity on the other is only small. This is the case in central Europe as well. It is not the fertile arable plains and the broad lowlands which are the most important areas for preserving biodiversity, but the coastal areas and the low mountain ranges, the river flood plains and Jurassic highlands as well as the lakes in northeastern and southern Germany. The streams in the low mountain ranges feature special species diversity. The geography of species-richness is sufficiently known, both globally and regionally, for us to be able to develop useful concepts and not merely to proceed following the old principle that we will protect whatever we can, even if the areas are minuscule. For protected areas to achieve their goals, they must fulfill all three significant criteria: they must be large enough, enable networking, and preserve representative segments of biotopes typical of the area with their individual worlds of life. Exactly the same is true at the continental and global scales.

Overfertilization

The second major reason for large losses of biodiversity in central Europe is overfertilization. It usually began in the 1970s. The amount of fertilizers, especially nitrogen compounds, that was applied to central European fields surpassed the amount of nutrients extracted by harvests quickly, within a decade or even less. Even by the early 1990s, the German Federal Agency for Nature Conservation determined that the average excess came to 104 kilograms of nitrogen per hectare per year for the entire country. Overfertilization was particularly pronounced in the regions with intensive agriculture. The entire northwestern part of Germany, from the Ruhr area to the North Sea and on eastwards to the Elbe River, as well as large parts of Bavaria, in particular the southeast, receive more than 150 kilograms, even more than 200 kilograms too much nitrogen per hectare and year. Roughly 100 kilograms surplus on average, for all of Germany, was calculated from these figures and those for the regions in the southwest and large areas of eastern Germany, where the nitrogen surpluses are significantly lower. Major urban areas, such as Berlin or Munich, stand out from the overall pattern of overfertilization. The nitrogen inputs in large cities are comparable to those in areas with only slight nitrogen pollution, such as parts of the Bavarian Forest, the Black Forest, the Palatinate Forest, and the Müritz region in Mecklenburg. There is a different reason for the fact that there are nitrogen inputs nonetheless in major cities and forests without agricultural use. After all, there are not only the direct inputs of fertilizers from agriculture in the form of mineral fertilizer and slurry which are responsible for these figures, but also nitrogen compounds which arrive by air.

In modern cogeneration plants, nitrogen from the air is also burned at high temperatures; the resulting compounds, called NOx, are then distributed across wide geographical areas by precipitation. Similar processes occur in the engines of motor vehicles traveling quickly, because at high engine speeds, nitrogen from the air is combusted as well. Ammonia (NH_3) from agriculture, which is released in gaseous form from ammonium compounds, is emitted into the air and is diffused in an uncontrolled manner via this path. In this way, nitrogen compounds that act as fertilizers are transported to places which are not supposed to be fertilized at all. In total, this 'fertilization from the air' amounts to between thirty and fifty kilograms of nitrogen per hectare and year (calculated in terms of pure nitrogen, not as a compound such as ammonium nitrate). Nitrogen input is intensified especially in the winter when cogeneration plants and domestic heating systems are run at full load. This nitrogen input alone is equivalent to total fertilization in agriculture as it was practiced through the middle of the twentieth century, but fertilization has increased by a factor of four or five since then. But although the use of mineral fertilizer for growing crops has not been increasing for roughly a decade, and although it is applied in a fairly targeted way when it is needed for the strongest period of growth, slurry is and remains a major and still increasing problem. In winter-cold areas with soil frost, it is applied three times, each of them the wrong time: in the spring, when the slurry tanks need emptying after the winter months; in the late autumn to empty the tanks before the onset of winter; and in between at the height of summer, when fields are available after harvesting. When livestock is put to pasture directly, however, most of the liquid and solid excretions end up on the pastures during the period of growth.

Taken together, mineral fertilizer, slurry, and unintended 'fertilization from the air' produce the excess of nutrients that benefits just a few species of plants one-sidedly, enables rampant growth, and creates cooler and (much) more damp living conditions near the ground than previously. This is true of the open landscape, but increasingly also of parks, woods, and protected areas. By far the largest part of species decline and loss over recent decades in central Europe can be traced back to this dual effect of agriculture: impoverishment of landscape structures and overfertilization. The latter affects the vast majority of small bodies of water, streams, and rivers. The groundwater carries the leachates from the fields and meadows to these bodies of water after heavy rainfalls and thaws. Fertilization from the air impairs the nutrient-poor heathland and areas with sandy soil as well as protected areas that are no longer cultivated; in the end, it damages all of central Europe, because it has become rare for more nutrients to be removed from the land areas than they receive due to general overfertilization. Large cities fare the best, relatively speaking, in the nutrient balance, because precipitation that acts as a fertilizer is rapidly conducted away via the sealed surface areas and the sewage system. In major cities, significantly higher temperatures – about 3°C and more – prevail than in the surrounding areas. This results in drier and nutrient-deficient conditions – which benefit biodiversity. We will return to the surprising phenomenon of particularly high species-richness in major cities below.

The Red List of Threatened Species express overfertilization and losses of structures in the open landscape very distinctly. In particular, species have disappeared ('extinct' in the area) which need nutrient-poor, open, and sunny habitats for survival. The many species that have similar needs or live in nutrient-poor wetlands, open woodland, bogs and exposed slopes or on heathlands are endangered. Protected areas become overgrown because they are overfertilized even without being cultivated. It is practically impossible to preserve larger nutrient-poor areas any-where in central Europe, except if very permeable and nutrient-poor sandy soils are available by nature.

In Bavaria, the endangered animal and plant species make up almost exactly half of the entire spectrum of animal and plant species. The direct and indirect consequences of agriculture account for between 70 and 95 percent of species loss, depending on which groups of species are taken into account. Agriculture is by far the largest cause of biodiversity loss and species extinction.

In comparison with agriculture, industry, settlement activities, and transportation are practically meaningless, because taken together they are responsible for only a few percent of biodiversity losses. Evidence that this is actually the case is provided by cities with their species-richness, which increases with city size, rather than decreasing with it, as one might expect. The few 'gains' on the part of species that benefit from overfertilization are not only insignificant in the total balance of species, but often concern real problem species. More on this in the following chapter.

Threats Posed By Alien Species

Alien species are currently considered one of the main threats to global biodiversity. This is doubtless the case on oceanic islands. The special adaptations which developed there in the course of millions of years are outcompeted by species that have been imported or introduced. The intruders sometimes wipe out indigenous species directly. For example, a few domestic cats running wild on small islands are enough to pose an extremely serious threat to the native birds that are not attuned to the pressure of predatory animals. Rats are particularly problematic because they are often active under the veil of darkness. The damage they cause is usually recognized too late for the rats to be successfully controlled and, if possible, eradicated. Goats have their own effects: they feed on the local vegetation to such an extent that the few indigenous species typical of an island disappear and make way for more resistant vegetation that usually comes from Europe, for instance, thistles. But where indigenous vegetation has been severely damaged or practically eradicated, the habitat for the animals that live there is no longer available. Thus, the natural world on islands is vulnerable by its very nature. The populations of plant and animal species are small, depending on how small the islands are and how much room there is in certain zones of altitude, for example on volcanoes.

Island species must be or must have been good colonizers by nature, otherwise they would not have succeeded in crossing great distances to arrive on the remote islands. That usually also means that they are less tough and weaker in competition than the mainland species. If mainland species arrive on the islands, their competitive power unfolds, sometimes in unimagined ways. They crowd out the endemic species, the ones that arrived earlier and adapted to the particular conditions on the island. Practically without exception, the perpetrator of this course of events has been mankind. Crop plants and domestic animals were transported on ships; by themselves, they never would have reached the islands. Other species often came along with them unnoticed, like stowaways. Human cultivation activities promoted the desired species as well as the unintentionally introduced ones settling in. The process of change got under way.

Unique species and habitats were annihilated in previous centuries. We have already mentioned the Hawaiian honeycreepers. Yet almost every island was and is affected, because barely a single one has been spared by people who have settled there in the desire to establish an independent lifestyle. Even if islands were deserted later, the imported and introduced species remained. In some cases, they could spread even more easily than in the presence of human beings who controlled them. For example, the goats marooned by pirates on the Galápagos Islands as suppliers of good meat for the pirates' occasional returns, became a major threat to these very special islands. Controlling the goats required a very large effort. On the larger islands, it was hardly possible to achieve a final victory because the goats became skittish and

withdrew to inaccessible areas. Because of the unique qualities of Galápagos, goats as well as other feral domestic animals
and introduced species were fought there especially vigorously.
On Galápagos, the issue was not only a single animal or plant
species that is a bit different from its mainland relations, but a
large-scale laboratory of evolution, so to speak, where the processes of species formation and adaptation can be observed in a
comprehensive and direct fashion. The appropriate means for
countermeasures were made available. People will continue to
have to fight off intruders which could alter the unique natural
world of Galápagos. Such an insight came too late for numerous
species on the Hawaiian Islands. They fell victim to human settlement; first by Polynesians who colonized this remote group
of islands in the Pacific, and then also the Americans who, as in
many other places in the Pacific, Americanized large portions of
the islands' natural worlds. In other places, it was the Europeans
who initiated and carried out such processes. In particular, they
Europeanized the largest island continent, Australia, to such a
degree that the southeast, with its temperate climate, and the
home of most of the population, corresponds more to British
conditions than the original Australian ones.

The invasion of the Europeans was followed by invasions of
European animal and plant species. Again, in addition to species
such as sheep and cattle, grain and vines, which were introduced
intentionally because they were considered economically indispensable, numerous species were imported for nostalgic reasons.
Eurasian skylarks from Europe were among them, as were
rabbits, which, in contrast to the skylarks, turned out to be a
major problem. In the dry and warm climate, which matched that
of their Iberian provenance perfectly, they multiplied so rapidly
that they became the main competition for the sheep; after all,
just like the sheep, the rabbits preferred the softer, tastier grass

to the hard, pointy spinifex. The watering holes that had been built for the sheep served the rabbits as well. The large kangaroos, which also competed with the sheep because their diets were similar, were much easier to bring down and decimate than the rabbits. Australia's infamous rabbit problem thus illustrates ideally to which extent Europeans could Europeanize a continent isolated for many millions of years, where the most independent evolutionary processes we know about took place, in a period of time as short as just two centuries – and with catastrophic consequences for the indigenous flora and fauna.

Making land suitable for cultivation is of particular importance in this context. Agricultural land is fertilized, thereby providing it with additional nutrients. This makes cultivated land attractive for many a species previously kept under control by scarcity. In any case, cultivation of land, regardless whether it occurred on islands or entire continents, reduced the land areas of untouched habitats with their special natural conditions. The loss of surface area alone, as we saw above, implies species loss. On the land areas newly subject to uses following European and American models, alien species were now able to spread and compete with the native species which had in any case already been forced to retreat. Therefore, their 'invasive potential' is supported in two ways, namely by pushing back the native species, which are weakened by the (severely) reduced numbers of plants or animals, and by strengthening the alien species, because quasi-native living conditions have been prepared for them on foreign soil. Fertilization is part of this second component, because the indigenous native species were adapted to the nutrient-poor living conditions. Where Australia's barren soils were meliorated and irrigated, it was practically inevitable that the European species newly introduced outcompeted the native species; just as in Europe, individual species with particularly high needs for nutrients have become the major beneficiaries of overfertilization and have appeared 'invasive' ever since.

For example, plants such as giant hogweed (*Heracleum mantegazzianum*) and Himalayan balsam (*Impatiens glandulifera*), both of which originated in the very nutrient-rich mountains of southwest Asia, grow up to two to three meters height in a single summer in overfertilized central Europe. The stalks of the giant hogweed can reach the thickness of one's lower arm, and are mostly hollow and not lignified. It shoots forth from a root-stalk, and for this reason, it achieves even more growth than the Himalayan Balsam, which germinates from seeds. Nonetheless, the Himalayan balsam also grows up to more than two meters height, full of juice and the lower parts of the stalks as thick as a finger, with dozens of large blossoms and multitudes of seeds to spread the species further. Both plants quickly develop vigorous stands which spread and found offshoots in other places, like colonies. They can do so because our lifestyle and management method release the amounts of nitrogen compounds they need to grow. In places where overfertilization is concentrated, such as ditches, streams, and moist edges of forests alongside overfertilized agricultural land, Himalayan balsam grows in pure stands, conspicuous because they are visible from a distance. Although bumblebees intensely frequent the large and very beautiful blossoms (which display all shades from deep red to pink to white with just the slightest red tinge) Himalayan balsam is considered an overly invasive alien species that should be controlled.

It has become invasive only since the 1970s, however, when the phenomenon of overfertilization struck. It had already existed in central Europe for more than a century, but had remained inconspicuous, as had the incomparably more problematic giant hogweed. It had been introduced by beekeepers in the nineteenth century to improve the yields of honey-producing plants. Giant hogweed blooms from the height of summer until late summer or early autumn, when the blossoms in the fields become very scarce. But, as we know well, only a few places in central Europe feature mass blossoming of heather. The large, plate-like, domed blossoms, many times the size of those of common hogweed (*Heracleum sphondylium*), the related indigenous species, attract numerous insects in addition to bees. One could see them in a positive light if giant hogweed did not cause one's skin to burn much more strongly than the original domestic species after touching the plant in sunlight. This so-called phototoxic effect is the main problem caused by giant hogweed. Similar to Himalayan balsam, it spreads wherever the soil is extremely rich in nitrogen compounds. Large areas which can be controlled only while wearing protective clothing can occur alongside highways, where mulched soils on cut slopes absorb and retain the nitrogen oxides formed when automobiles are driven at high speeds, creating the ideal growing ground for the giant plant. Stands of giant hogweed also develop in nutrient-rich peripheries of cities, on railroad embankments, and near fences of gardens fertilized too heavily. In settled areas, the danger is particularly high that children and adults who are unaware of the dangers of touching this plant get burned severely and suffer lasting pain. The skin's allergic reactions are different from the response to touching stinging nettles. They are more like the reactions of people allergic to bee poison after being stung by a bee.

What characterizes these two plants, the currently most-discussed 'invasive plants' in central Europe, basically applies to all invasive species, regardless whether they are 'alien' or 'indigenous.' They can become invasive if the conditions have been created for them to do so. Practically without exception, they arrive in the wake of human beings and then spread. Almost always, their invasiveness is limited to the world of mankind, in other words, the cultivated landscape. Invasive species hardly enter habitats that have remained sufficiently natural, if they enter them at all. Their success depends on mankind. Where man has simplified nature and transformed it according to his purposes, their powers can unfold. When human beings change their management methods, the invasive plants are beaten back, or they disappear.

This is illustrated perfectly by a water plant that was widely known decades ago, made headlines, and actually induced major costs: Canadian pondweed (*Elodea canadensis*). When in the 1950s and 1960s, municipal wastewater was full of phosphates from detergents, the plant grew en masse, clogged canals, and interfered with shipping. Nitrogen compounds from agricultural fertilizers were increasingly washed into the bodies of water. Thus, the two most important substances for the growth of water plants were overabundant in the water. The water plant, originating from North America, probably spread from aquariums. Under such beneficial circumstances, the decorative aquarium plant whose growth was easy to control developed into a plague. It had not attracted much attention in the waters of its North American home because there was no overfertilization with phosphates and nitrogen compounds there. When detergents were made phosphate-free and practically all homes were connected to wastewater treatment plants, the incidences of the water plague in Germany fell off sharply. By now, the once so invasive species is barely to be found.

Its example shows to what extent invasiveness is directly controlled by mankind – but also that it certainly is possible to take appropriate countermeasures. Therefore, alien species threaten the 'native' ones, however native they may actually be, only to a small degree wherever the natural composition of the spectrum of species and their abundances have remained semi-natural.

Alien species are doubtless a greater risk on islands than on continents. In areas that have been under cultivation for centuries or millennia, they are part of the dynamic that changes the flora and fauna of the cultivated land. Economic damages should be considered as such, regardless whether they are caused by native or (currently still) alien species.

The same applies to the communication and spread of pathogens. Concerning diseases, the primary issue is the relative frequency of incidence. Alien species can and will become problematic only if they have become common enough, that is, as common as or more common than the corresponding native species. Raccoon dogs (*Nyctereutes procyonides*) cannot be classified as a risk a priori just because they are spreading to central Europe from the east, as long as comparable small predators such as foxes, badgers, martens, but also domesticated dogs and cats are incomparably more abundant and must therefore also be taken into consideration as carriers and vectors of diseases specific to predatory animals. Our view of 'the foreigners' can turn into a negative stereotype all too quickly and shift towards an atmosphere of xenophobia.

It is not permissible to simply generalize from a few examples that are more or less justified. Alien species are or become truly problematic only when they drive back or threaten to annihilate native, that is, endemic species in particular. Then they become meaningful in terms of preserving biodiversity. This danger is present to an incomparably greater extent on (small) islands and possibly also on fragments of semi-natural conditions than it is in the usual cultivated landscape. As a cultivated landscape is always very different from the original natural state, we need to weigh the pros and cons particularly carefully before making a decision and adopting countermeasures. After all, as we know, yesteryear's 'aliens' have become today's natives which we would not like to dispense with, especially in the cultural landscape. For instance, should we do without cornflowers (*Centaurea cyanus*) and red poppies (*Papaver rhoeas*), chamomile (*Matricaria chamomillae*) and all the many other field weeds just because they were immigrants and aliens centuries ago? They were controlled as weeds until the recent past. And what about skylarks? Or the many, many other animals and plants that came to our part of the world centuries ago? The European cultural landscapes would be very species-poor and monotonous if not for the immigrants from times past. They contributed quite significantly to the fact that the cultural landscapes, that is, the well-kept and variegated landscapes, not the cleared-out and monotonous ones, are considered to be so beautiful that people want to preserve or preferably even recreate them. Preserving (old) cultural landscapes is one of nature protection's stated goals. It dovetails seamlessly with the esthetic goal of preserving scenic beauties that includes many a special species of animal and plant. They are to be preserved for their beauty – in this country as well as globally. The beauties need not play a 'major role in the ecological balance.'

Persecution

To be honest, the Darwin's finches and mockingbirds of the Galápagos Islands are not as beautiful as birds of paradise. The sea lions cannot contend with the spectacular lions of the Serengeti, either. The bizarre marine iguanas appear primeval, the giant tortoises attract attention mostly because of their provocative slowness. Nonetheless, all of them, and all the other species of animals on the Galápagos Islands, are very special. Certainly most of them occur only there, on the volcanic islands roughly a thousand kilometers west of South America on the equator, islands that look extremely inhospitable, like lunar landscapes, when viewed from the sea. In other words, they are endemic species. But endemic species are to be found on other oceanic islands as well; in any case, totaling many more than on Galápagos. The animals of these 'enchanted islands,' Islas Encantadas, as they are called in Spanish, have something else to thank for their uniqueness. In the seclusion of these islands, the fauna has retained a 'sense of basic trust' towards human beings which larger animals practically everywhere else have lost entirely or to a large extent. This is because human beings persecuted them. Although man is not a predatory animal by biological nature, he is by far the most dangerous enemy of practically all mammals, birds, and other animals that reach a particular size. Wild animals have learned by experience to conceive of man as an enemy. Human beings are considered particularly dangerous. The animals flee or retreat into the dark of night to protect their vital activities. Which is a good idea. Human beings are the animals' greatest and most threatening enemy.

Even if, as in Germany, 99% of human beings are harmless, animals could still fall victim to the small fraction remaining. Native deer are very skittish for most of the year, in any case for the duration of the hunting season. Birds such as ducks and geese that migrate across long distances retain this skittishness year-round and for their whole lives. Even if they might be protected in one country and have nothing to fear, this does not necessarily apply as well in all the other countries through which they migrate. Hunters believe that wild animals must be 'wild,' that is, skittish. The fact that this is by no means necessarily the case by nature is shown in television documentaries or experience in far-away national parks and wild animal reserves. Not even their behavior towards the large predators is as nervous as it is towards human beings. In the national parks of eastern Africa, zebras, gnus, and gazelles permit approaching lions to pass through their herds as if through a corridor without panicking. They can assess whether lions are out for prey or not, and what they might be looking for. Hunters' guns cannot be evaluated in the same way. Their deadly effect goes way beyond the normal distances that animals of prey have to keep in relation to their natural enemies for safety. If a bird has sufficient physical stamina, it can brace itself even for the breakneck plummet, fast as a bullet, of a falcon attacking it – and the chances of escaping are not bad at all. The success rates achieved by predatory animals and birds of prey when hunting are so poor that at first, researchers could hardly believe their findings. Only one attack in ten is successful – at most. Even if one in three were successful, that would mean that two out of three possible victims would get away and be able to learn from the experience. Not so in the case of deadly shots from afar or underhanded methods of capture such as snare traps or trapping pits, not to mention poisoned bait. Only the most skittish and cautious survive such human and inhumane persecution.

The consequences are to be observed in the animals' behavior. The hunted mammals and birds are quite disproportionately nervous. This shyness keeps them from settling in many suitable places where they could certainly live on the natural resources and raise their young – for the simple reason that people are active there. After all, these animals must be wary of all human beings in order to be able to escape those who truly pose a danger to them. Only a few species have the level of skills and ability to learn that enable them to differentiate the few truly dangerous people from the large majority of harmless humans. The crow family of birds, for example, belongs to this group, above all the common raven (Corvus corax). They learn to recognize human beings individually and differentiate them from other ones – to the displeasure of hunters, where they go after ravens or their smaller and much more common relatives, the carrion crow (*Corvus corone*). These few exceptions do not change the basic fact: the image of man as an enemy works. It is passed on from generation to generation. Reducing hunted animals' wild behaviour takes a long time and requires real protection in national parks, not merely parks labeled as reserves. Only there can visitors observe animals' natural behavior, which is otherwise hidden from their view.

Anyone who has experienced a mockingbird – an inconspicuous gray bird, roughly the size and shape of a slender blackbird – trying to extract a shoelace from his shoe while he was busy changing a roll of film, for example, will be impressed by such behavior. But if a sea lion gives birth right next to the path that visitors may use, but must not leave, and looks the astounded human beings in the face with big, dark eyes, then almost any human being must feel nothing less than shame about what we have done to the animals that this sense of basic trust has been lost. The sea lion's eyes do not reflect even the slightest fear of the creatures surrounding her as she gives birth, creatures entirely different from her.

Once the sea lions have lost their strong sense of fear, human beings are regarded practically in the same way as cows, so harmless that in this part of the world, starlings land on their backs and storks stride alongside them in order to catch insects. But this comparison does not capture the essence of the phenomenon. Although storks and starlings naturally classify grazing cows 'correctly' because they are accustomed to them, on the Galápagos Islands, birds and mammals such as sea lions take a positive interest in human beings. They approach them, take a look at these strange creatures, bobbing and weaving around them in the water. When we swim and dive with sea lions or fur seals, we can hardly avoid the impression that these elegant swimmers marvel at the funny movements we make.

Safari tourists in national parks in eastern African experience large animals in a similar way, for example, when cheetahs use the cars as lookouts, lions lie down in the vehicles' shade to escape the heat, or other large animals approach curiously. One can also make friends with wild boars; the animals can recognize a particular human being with absolute certainty and differentiate that person from everyone else. Even our European robins (*Erithacus rubecula*) sometimes display such curiosity. Individual ones come closer, to barely an arm's length, and listen to people talking to them. If one returns to the same place several days later, the robin will be there right away, too. We have come to know that all kinds of small birds in city parks become hand-tame and pick seeds from our palms, as chickadees or nuthatches do. In any case, cities provide many prime examples for changes in animals' behavior when they have lost their skittishness and no longer consider human beings to be disturbing or enemies. Otherwise suspicious foxes bask in the sun on someone's terrace, build their dens by the garage, and play with their young in the garden. Water birds that live in the wild and by no means eat out of people's hands, such as decorative common mergansers (*Mergus merganser*), can be best observed performing their courtship displays on urban bodies of water in the late winter and spring. Uninhibited, beavers (*Castor fiber*) permit people to watch them fell young willows on the banks of rivers or nibble the bark off of twigs – and so forth.

Hinduism, one of humankind's great civilizations, deserves the highest rank in mankind's way of dealing with animals. At a population of a billion, the Indian subcontinent is the most populous place on Earth after China – and also one of the richest in animals. Most animals, mammals as well as birds and many others, enjoy respect and esteem that protect them as living creatures. For practically all species, skittishness is not a problem as there is no need for such behavior. Even though it is a densely-populated and not exactly affluent country, India affords the 'luxury' of large animals classified as dangerous, such as tigers (*Panthera tigris*) and leopards (*Panthera pardus*), wolves, giant snakes, and crocodiles.

It was the Europeans who eradicated the most animals by direct persecution. Almost all mammals and larger birds that lived on islands fell victim to their blind trust when European seafarers came and took possession of the islands. Nowhere else are the larger animals as skittish as in the direct sphere of influence of Europeans and their descendants. The few exceptions from the most recent past prove the rule. For instance, white-tailed deer (*Odocoileus virginianus*) *in North America move to urban gardens at the onset of the (relatively short) hunting season and wait there in safety until the danger has passed*. It is most remarkable that is not the poorest of the poor who have eradicated the most species, but the wealthiest. This must make us conclude that those who have caused the most extinction, both today and previously, must make the greatest contribution towards preserving Earth's biological diversity. It was and still is the 'western lifestyle' that has caused the greatest damage to nature and the most significant species losses. For this reason, the resulting obligations for the future are distributed quite unevenly across the globe. The greatest contribution by far is to be made by no one but us.

6 Rescuing Biodiversity

Cities: The Great Unplanned Experiment

Humanity and nature are mutually exclusive. At least, their coexistence fails when the numbers of humans grow too large. Then, nature is left without any space. Plants and animals withdraw, become rare, and die out – locally, then regionally, and, in the end, altogether. Roughly speaking, this sums up the view of many people who are concerned about the preservation of the earth's biodiversity. Long since the single dominant species on the planet, the spreading human population is having catastrophic impacts on nature. A large part of the earth's biodiversity will inevitably perish as humanity continues to grow. After many years of intensive effort, of on-the-ground, body-and-mind struggle against rapidly expanding human settlement, against industry and transport, conservationists have become dispirited. An apocalyptic mood has taken hold. Small wonder when even in wealthy nations like Germany, indeed in the state of Bavaria, with its leading economic performance and strong cultural reputation, the Red List of Threatened Species cannot claim success.

A study undertaken by the Bavarian Environment Agency as recently as 2003 showed that half of all animal and plant species living in the wild in Bavaria are endangered. In light of this result, thirty years of species protection in a state whose great nature is such a source of pride – indeed, a basis for tourism – would appear to have been fruitless. The findings were so negative because Bavaria is a state dominated by broad, open expanses of woods and meadows – agricultural landscapes where rates of species endangerment run high.

While it is understandable, the growing pessimism is nonetheless not entirely warranted. The situation is not hopeless. There have been highly remarkable, if nearly unnoticed, successes – for the most part unplanned. The most unusually promising findings come from precisely those places that were expected to be the end of nature: big cities. Wherever they have been studied closely, they have proven not only surprisingly species-rich, but in some respects even to be the last refuge of many threatened species. There are abundant examples of this. Among the German states, Hamburg can, in contrast to Bavaria, boast highly positive results. The spectrum of large cities with notable and valuable species richness ranges from cosmopolitan centers like New York, London, Berlin, and Singapore to million-plus metropolises such as Munich and Hamburg, to smaller cities like Anchorage, Alaska. The many studies made in the last thirty-some years of the incidence and abundance of plant and animal species living in the wild concur with extensive research into urban ecology which finds (1) that, in relation to their land area, cities are considerably above average in species richness, and (2) that species richness does not decrease, but rather increases with the size of the city. Cities often harbor species which have become quite rare, and which fare better in the protective company of human populations than in the surrounding countryside. One set of findings on species richness in German cities is shown in Figure 12.

The strength of this increase in species variety of course depends on the structure of the city. Densely built cities with concentrations of skyscrapers are naturally far less suited to wild

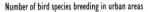

Number of bird species breeding in urban areas

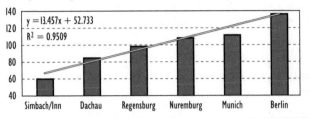

$y = 13.457x + 52.733$
$R^2 = 0.9509$

Figure 12 In Central Europe, the number of bird species breeding in
urban areas rises sharply as the size of the city increases

Two-thirds of all bird species reproducing in Germany breed in Berlin's urban
area

animals and plants than those in which built-up areas intermesh
with non-urbanized surrounding areas, and where there are large
parks and urban waters. In this respect, Berlin serves as a very
positive example, lacking only true hills and the sea. (Marine
animal and plant species do reach Hamburg's urban area.)

On closer observation, wooded areas in some cities even prove
significantly 'better' than forests in the countryside, as wood production does not have priority and many old hollow trees remain
standing. The alternation of old stands with new growth and the
presence of glades and meadows (including those for people's
use) make urban woods structurally more diverse than economic
forests outside cities. Similarly, urban land and waters usually
do not serve purposes of productive agriculture or fishing. And
provided they are not extremely densely built, cities' structural
variety itself strongly promotes species richness. As previously
discussed, however, two further basic conditions must be met for
such species richness to come about: only minimal fertilization,
or at least no overfertilization; and little or no persecution of

larger mammal and bird species. Cities usually fulfill and sometimes guarantee both of these conditions. With the exception of
garden allotments, neither chemical fertilizer nor liquid manure
is spread over large areas in cities. They therefore constitute
'nutrient-poor green islands' in the sea of Central Europe's massively overfertilized agricultural lands. And because animals are
rarely hunted or harassed in the city, they tend not to become
skittish around humans, but in fact rather bolder.

All over the world, this brings about unexpected situations.
An obviously healthy fox, for example, can roam Berlin in broad
daylight undisturbed, without arousing suspicion of carrying
rabies. Moose and black bears, and even grizzly bears, wander
trustfully through the residential yards and streets of Anchorage,
Alaska. Moose calves must be freed occasionally from yards surrounded by fences that they, unlike their mothers, cannot simply
jump over. Hares sit by the runways of the Frankfurt airport,
unperturbed by the giant birds thundering past them and taking
off. Blackbirds take parked railroad cars as breeding grounds,
and their natural enemies, sparrow hawks, nest in trees just a
few feet from the windows of hospitals. The shy peregrine falcon
has found safe nesting places on the Cologne Cathedral, Berlin's
city hall, and the towers of power plants. Both species of indigenous marten – the stone or beech marten (*Martes foina*) and the
pine or sweet marten (*Martes martes*) – live in higher concentrations in Göttingen and other cities than they do in surrounding
wooded or farm country. The beech marten's propensity to bite
through cables and hoses in car engines has not led to eradication campaigns like those in the countryside when a marten raids
a henhouse, even though the damage to the cars is many times
higher than the value of a few slaughtered chickens. German
farmers are paid for such losses, whether substantial or not. This
system of compensation for damage caused by wild animals is

solidly established – in the countryside. City dwellers are not eligible; no compensation exists for urban gardeners whose allotments are targeted for an early harvest by marauding wild boars.

The animal world of large cities indeed comprises a large part of the so-called wild-living species. Beavers (*Castor fiber* in Europe and *Castor canadensis* in North America) live in cities if the rivers that flow through them offer suitable opportunity. The hollows of old trees or unused cellars and catacombs offer the best dwellings for bats. Berlin's urban area is home to around 1,000 of the best singers in Europe's bird world, nightingales. This is roughly as many or perhaps even more than are still found in all of Bavaria. Studies show that the plethora of butterfly species in cities, above all among the particularly species-rich nocturnal moth groups, is comparable to that in nature reserves. These findings are an expression of one of the three basic requirements for the conservation and development of biodiversity, as previously mentioned: limited fertilizing of the biotopes in the cities. Within cities, nutrient-poor, dry and warm areas are often distributed in a mosaic-like manner, while outside the cities 100 kilograms of nitrogen and more have been added to the soil per hectare annually for decades.

However, species variety not only increases with the size of the city (qualifying Berlin or Hamburg as especially rich in species), but has also developed positively in recent years. Whereas the diversity of bird, wild plant and insect species is in (sharp) decline in areas of open fields and, in part, forest, it is on the increase in the cities. Wherever comparable studies from earlier periods are available, this finding emerges. For instance, while the urban area of Berlin lost a dozen bird species during the last quarter of the nineteenth century, it gained more than this number a century later, between 1960 and 2000. Thus the city is clearly richer in species than it was one hundred years ago. The greatest numbers of wild plant species are typically reached in residential areas when these include disturbed sites and parks. At the edge of cities there is a clear drop-off in biodiversity, as was shown in the cases of both Berlin and Nuremberg at the end of the twentieth century. For butterflies and, to an even greater degree, wild plants, even city centers prove richer in species than open agricultural land where monocultures are grown. This can be seen at a glance, though we typically do not want to believe it. Wheat and corn fields are meant to produce grain, not wildflowers and butterflies. Inner-urban areas are free of any such production demand. A meadow in a city park that does not 'have to produce" anything may in fact provide habitat for a profusion of different butterflies, wild bees, grasshoppers and other small animals, as well as colorful flowers. Urban gardeners' differing visions as to what should grow and thrive in their gardens automatically gives rise to a diverse and unplanned mix. The combination of gardens and parks – the tree stock of which dates to times when 'native" and 'non-native" were far less important than 'beautiful" and 'fitting" – results in species variety that exceeds the natural maximum to be expected. Some large cities may be richer in different tree species per 100 square kilometers than are tropical rainforests.

The plant species that inhabit residential gardens in Central Europe outnumber those in the wild by a factor of two to three. Whether this diversity should be considered 'unnatural' or simply a part of developments that have been unfolding for centuries in cultivated landscapes is the subject of fierce debate. Taking the global view of the preservation of species variety, it is certainly of secondary significance whether the beautiful cornflower (originally a non-native species brought here with agriculture) survives in the cultivated landscape of Central Europe, or in its native region, where some species are more threatened by changes in the local landscape than they are here. And should all of the peregrine falcon's 'natural' breeding grounds be lost, leaving it only nesting sites on church spires and city halls, this is clearly preferable to the species dying out. Species conservation and 'naturalness' do not necessarily have to go together.

Preserving natural habitats in a state as free from direct human influence as possible is one of the two greatest aims of nature conservation efforts. This generally can only be realized in nature reserves, which will be discussed in the following section of this chapter. However, the conservation of species can also be achieved largely independently of nature reserves. If birds that feed on fish, such as herons and mergansers, do better around urban waters than in rural areas, why should this not be allowed to play a role in their preservation? It is frequently forgotten in our consideration of cities that the condition of the country-side, the cultivated land, is also far from its natural state. The European hare (*Lepus europaeus*), the gray partridge (*Perdix perdix*) and many other species of the open land, including its plant world, would hardly be able to live, if at all, without this human-cultivated Central European landscape. The fact that the cities have long since become areas of retreat for some of the species that are typical of these open lands is an expression of their dependency on humans – in both positive and negative respects.

Cities and towns, industrial facilities, and other land developed for technical purposes comprise around 10% of Central Europe's total land area. They rank third behind farm lands and forests, and far ahead of nature reserves. In land area, territory inhabited by humans exceeds that of nature reserves by five to ten times on average. This gives human settlements great significance as habitat for wild species. Thus the surprisingly good findings and mostly positive developments are occasion to hope that the cities will increasingly provide impulses in support of the preservation of natural biodiversity. The urban population often develops a greater understanding of nature than do people who must live directly from the land and its productivity. This is not surprising. Owners and managers of woodlands look at the forest in terms of the timber yield, and much less with an eye to the protection of beetle species that need dead trees to live. The positive attitude of the urban population is expressed in the considerable amounts of money, primarily in the form of donations, that flow into both national and international nature conservation. Without these donations, organizations such as the WWF and the Frankfurt Zoological Society would not be able to realize their superb conservation projects. Through this support, the population demonstrates the value it places on conservation efforts.

Nature Reserves: Islands Of Refuge?

The world has the Frankfurt Zoological Society and the personal dedication of Bernhard Grzimek in the 1960s and 1970s to thank for wonderful national parks in eastern Africa, such as the Serengeti. The film titled 'Serengeti Must Not Die," made by Grzimek with his son Michael, who lost his life in a plane crash during the shooting, is considered a turning point in the history of nature protection, just as Rachel Carson's book 'Silent Spring" rang in the age of environmental protection. The reactions of people – of millions of people – bestowed a value on nature previously unknown or unaccepted at least in Western societies.

The first national parks in the US had already ushered in this process in the late nineteenth century. Subsequently, concerns for protecting the natural heritage spurred the development of nature protection in Germany as well as other European countries. Many approaches of modern-day nature protection are still linked to the concept of heritage as well. Germany's Nature Protection Act of 1938 demarcated 98 areas in which nature was to be protected and granted priority over other interests. These were the first real nature reserves in Germany. Over time, the number of nature reserves multiplied, but their total area did not grow by much; when East and West Germany were unified in 1990, the total area of nature reserves in West Germany had just doubled. The nature reserves in East Germany, both large and magnificent, amounted to a phenomenal gain. Aside from them, especially such complexes as the Müritz area or the Schorfheide, which are big enough to offer effective protection, most of the nature reserves in inland Germany remain islands too small to secure species-richness. According to the relationship between species-richness and size of land area, almost a third of Germany's land area would have to be protected well enough to achieve the goal of preserving at least 90 percent of the species present here in the long term.

Surprisingly, only a very few species have disappeared in recent decades ('extinct' in Germany), even though protected areas make up just over 1% of former West Germany and a few percent of former East Germany. Theory and findings seem to contradict one another. But that is not the case. After all, nature reserves alone would in all likelihood actually not have been able to preserve Germany's species-richness in the absence of areas such as military training areas, some forest areas, and also areas settled by people where species survive because good populations continue to exist. If we take nature reserves, military training areas, forests, and cities together, they make up more than 40% of the total land area. In principle, this can secure species-richness in Central Europe, provided there are no fundamental changes, for example in the forests. These counterweights collectively make the species losses in the agrarian landscape, which constitutes about 55% of the land area, bearable to some extent. But in concrete terms, it also means that outside of nature reserves, protection of species is granted outstanding importance in Germany as well as in other European countries. In densely populated countries, nature protection cannot be limited to reserves alone, because practically without fail, they are too small and too far apart to sustain the coherence of the populations of endangered species whose numbers have declined. For this reason, concrete protection of species is required which is not related only to specific tracts of land. All the same, it cannot replace protection by means of reserves. After all, even in light of the diversity of species in cities, forests and military training areas, numerous animal and plant species need the special living conditions that exist only in the designated reserves. A raised bog cannot also be a major city. A wooded cemetery or tree-rich residential areas of a city, on the other hand, can by all means offer many elements of the habitat that animals and plants need which would otherwise live in open woodland.

In small reserves, a major problem usually arises: because of their small size, the various land uses conflict with one another, uses which would certainly be sustainable and could be retained if the reserves were large enough. In most Central European reserves for aquatic birds, it cannot be tolerated that people go fishing or practice other recreational activities without restrictions during the brooding season. The nest losses due to the disturbances would be too large. And a policy of continuing to permit hunting without restrictions while nature lovers are locked out because they could disturb the animals can be reconciled neither with the conservation goals nor with the aims of the general public. The smaller the reserves, the more rigorously the land uses must be separated and restricted to achieve the goal of protection. Conflicts are unavoidable when trade-offs have to be found which involve one party that cannot tolerate (human) compromises. If aquatic birds' hatch is disturbed, it makes no difference whether the disturbance was caused by fisherman who had the right to frequent the reserve during the most sensitive period or by nature lovers who did not have that right as they would have needed exceptional permission. The fact that neither group 'wanted' to disturb the birds is of no use to them if they have lost their young. Even if all is not well in some countries' nature reserves in this respect, major successes can be observed nonetheless.

The nature reserves of some private organizations, such as the British Royal Society for the Protection of Birds (RSPB, see 'Remarkable Successes', below) can serve as models in every respect. But those nature reserves, too, in which it is not necessary to pay much heed to disturbances are especially instructive. The world-famous Keoladeo Ghana Bird Sanctuary in Bharatpur in India, not far from the even more renowned Taj Mahal, fills most bird lovers who have traveled there from Europe with utter wonder. Herons and storks, ducks and geese, as well as the sublimely beautiful cranes–visitors on small dams or boats can observe and photograph practically all the birds from unbelievably close up. The birds do not need to be skittish because there is no threat to them there. It is the larger animals' nervousness that spoils the opportunity for visitors to experience impressive species in many nature reserves in Germany. Some visitors even come to think that there are hardly any animals in Germany's national parks, but only landscape that is to be viewed as like stage set. Even if the number of animals is much smaller than it could be if they were not skittish, they do in fact exist. But the ones that are there keep in hiding for good reason. And that is why reducing fear and opening up nature reserves for nature lovers under appropriate conditions are among the central tasks of the relevant administrations or organizations. Only then will the nature reserves be in a position to fulfill their intended tasks, which is what the general public usually also expects of them. Even small reserves can yield successes if the animals there do not have to be nervous. Urban water bodies, with the safety they provide for aquatic birds, are the model for areas and cultures where larger animals are hunted and chased.

But there is another aspect which should be placed at the top of the list, taking a global perspective. Preserving the species-richness of the earth requires a system of nature reserves that assigns top priority to securing the centers of biodiversity – the hot spots. Only rarely do the necessity of protection and the actually realized amount of it coincide as well as on the Galápagos Islands. Tourism to these remote islands ensures protection by means of the income it generates, but it must be managed, or quotas must be imposed with regard to the carrying capacity of the islands. In some respects, the situation is similar concerning the wonderful tropical character of the Seychelles in the Indian Ocean where high-class, partly luxury tourism guarantees the preservation of the unique wildlife of these islands, minuscule in comparison with Galápagos.

Focal points of biodiversity, such as innermost Amazonia on the eastern edge of the Andes or practically inaccessible mountain forests in Southeast Asia between Burma, China, and Cambodia have no chance of eco-tourism that would both support the people living there, giving them prospects for the future, and sustain the special natural environment there. The concept of national parks works where people can experience truly superb natural features. It will endure even in Africa, despite the economic and societal problems there. It will be easier to explain to poor people in Tanzania that the Ngorongoro Crater with its fabulous scenery and its large animals and the Serengeti with its lions and buffalo, millions of gnus and hundreds of thousands of zebras are truly special parts of their world, and therefore belong to its national and cultural heritage. After all, they can observe how many people from all over the world travel there for this reason, and in doing so, also improve their own living conditions. The Colombian farmers who plant coca will not be readily convinced by someone pointing out to them that there are particularly rare, possibly still undiscovered frogs, beetles, or bugs in the mountain forests which they want to use for planting. The positive approaches evident around the globe of creating thousands upon thousands of nature reserves must therefore be supported in a much more massive way reaching far beyond pure eco-tourism. After all, eco-tourism will continue to be concentrated on the spectacular areas and landscapes which may not have particular relevance for preserving biodiversity rather than the hot spots in which only connoisseurs of the relevant animals and plants will find exciting things to see or discover. Today, the latter is increasingly being curtailed, because the countries in question fear that the scientists who come to examine the biodiversity of their natural areas will exploit their country, merely in a different way than the colonial rulers of yore, and take the secrets they discover back home for economic exploitation. The more distrustful people are of research, the less it will be possible to preserve or protect otherwise 'uninteresting areas.'

Germany cannot be proud of its track record in this regard when it comes to the state of research on and access to nature reserves and national parks. They exclude people with a real interest in nature to a much greater degree than they limit previous uses detrimental to the goal of protection. These uses are continued because agriculture and forestry, hunting and fishing are exempted as a matter of principle from the restrictions due to nature protection. The German system of nature protection makes it much more difficult to 'exclude' or substantially limit people who can claim previous rights to use the land than to restrict the rights of those who cannot. Anyone whose attempts to obtain special approval to enter a water body designated as a bird sanctuary have failed need only join the local fishing association, and from then on, special approval is no longer required. Government ordinances regulating nature reserves are full of bans. Almost without exception, they concern only nature-lovers. The fact that nature protection does not rate highly with the overwhelming majority of the population and is considered more a curse than a necessity is due to this system.

The problems associated with it can indeed be solved, and the best way to do so would be by means of a private system of nature reserves, such as those of the Royal Society for the Protection of Birds in the United Kingdom or the Audubon Society in the US. If all the rights to use the land, such as hunting, fishing, or forestry, belong to the private nature protection society, there will be no more conflicts due to the need to reconcile interests, and the nature reserve can be oriented towards the protection goals in the best possible manner. Such a system of private nature reserves is more than overdue and indispensable in many countries if nature protection is to be anchored more firmly in society.

Remarkable Successes

Millions of people are members of nature protection societies. Individuals of the highest international renown are committed to nature protection. Crowned heads are patrons or honorary chairs of bird protection associations; the Royal Society for the

Protection of Birds (RSPB) in the United Kingdom, for example, can truly call itself 'royal' with its membership numbering more than one million. Prince Bernhard of the Netherlands and Prince Philip of Great Britain chaired the WWF. Peter Scott, the co-founder of one of the most effective systems for protecting bio-diversity – called the Ramsar Convention for the city of Ramsar in Iran, where the convention was signed – was knighted because of his achievements for protecting aquatic birds. International nature protection has him to thank for its most well-known symbol, the panda bear in the WWF's logo.

During the times when communist states such as the Soviet Union and China were still mostly closed to Westerners, con-servationists were able to obtain access and initiate protection of the giant panda. In the former Soviet Union, specialists for protecting water birds were received and treated like high-level guests of state. In Africa's zones of unrest, personalities such as Jane Goodall, Dian Fossey and numerous other conservation-ists accomplished nothing less than the incredible for preserv-ing chimpanzees, gorillas, rhinoceroses, elephants, and other animals. Our closest relatives, the chimpanzees and gorillas, were liberated from their image as wild beasts and have become sought-after creatures; people book special and expensive trips to gaze at them as if they were a mirror of humankind. We have also been successful, in spite of many difficulties, in rescuing great whales from the threat of total extinction. A few examples selected from numerous successes in protecting biodiversity will illustrate this in the following pages.

For instance, the gray whale (*Eschrichtius robustus*), one of the medium-sized great whales at a length of up to fifteen meters and weight of more than thirty metric tons, had almost been wiped out in the early twentieth century. Whalers slaughtered these giants on a massive scale , when they entrapped themselves in the lagoons of Baja California. In these Mexican lagoons, where there has been whale-watching tourism for decades, the gray whales mate and give birth to their young. Three large shallow lagoons are the major part of the gray whales' winter quarters. In the spring, they migrate from there to the North Pacific, especially the Bering Sea, where they forage all summer long. In the autumn, they migrate back south to the lagoons along the west coast of North America. Canada, the US, and Mexico have placed the gray whale under protection. Since 1946, their stocks have been increasing again slowly, but continually. Forty years later, in the 1980s, around 16,000 gray whales were counted. Many of these giants permit whale watchers in inflatable dinghies to observe them from very close up in the lagoons. Again and again, some whales even swim directly to the boats and permit people to touch them or remove barnacles (a type of crustacean) from to their skin. It is surely one of the deepest impressions nature lovers can have to peer into the eye of such a whale from less than a meter's distance, and to see themselves mirrored there.

In the meantime, there are various places for watching whales: off Hawaii and the western Australian coast, Punta Arenas in Argentina, and Madeira in the Atlantic as well as the west and east coasts of North America. Tours usually take visitors to see humpback whales (*Megaptera novaeangliae*) because they swim very slowly and are especially tolerant.'The remaining stocks are also multiplying and have grown from an estimated 7,000 in the early 1980s to more than 10,000. The example of the gray whale is particularly instructive. Because gray whales live in very close proximity to the coasts, it was possible to rescue them from annihilation by just three countries cooperating, for they rarely swim out into international waters. Their fellow whales in the North Atlantic did not fare as well. In the late eighteenth century, they were exterminated completely. The odds continue to be against the last of the West Pacific gray whales that migrate along the coasts from Kamchatka to Korea and had multiplied in the lagoons there. The resolutions of the International Whaling Commission (IWC) brought about further successes, even if countries such as Norway and Japan, which certainly do not rank among the poor countries, did not want to 'afford' ending whaling. By now, the whalers from there are both restricted and observed so closely that they no longer pose an acute threat of extermination to great whales. The largest animal that ever lived, as far as we know, the blue whale (*Balaenoptera musculus*), will also probably survive as international regulations for protection have come into force. Commercial whaling had decimated stocks from an estimated more than a quarter of a million to just a few thousand individuals.

People are very fond of dolphins, the smaller relatives of the great whales. Currently, however, the unique Yangtze river dolphin or Baiji (*Lipotes vexillifer*) is apparently dying out in spite of all efforts to protect it, even though this blind river dolphin has been protected rigorously in China since 1975. This would be the first larger mammal to become extinct in the three-quarters of a century since the demise of the Tasmanian wolf (*Thylacinus cynocephalus*), which was seen last in the 1930s. The situation is also precarious for the other species of river dolphin, which are practically trapped – with the possible exception of those which inhabit the Amazon. The dolphins and small cetaceans that live in the oceans have better chances for survival; tuna fishing, which killed many dolphins unintentionally, has been improved, at least in some areas. Keeping dolphins and occasionally even the much larger orcas (*Orcinus orca*) in large ocean aquariums (dolphinariums) has given the popularity of these doubtless highly intelligent marine mammals a strong boost.

On balance, the cramped living conditions and the deaths of mammals in dolphinariums have been worthwhile for the species as a whole, as tragic as they have been in each particular case. This applies in a comparable way for large land mammals that are kept and bred in zoos. Preserving tigers in the jungle or in the deep woods of North East Asia is a challenge for the protection of species, surely one of the most difficult challenges of all. After all, these big cats are dangerous for humans as well, and they need very large spaces in which they can live. They require at least ten times as much space per individual animal, compared with lions in East Africa. The fact that the tiger as a species still survives in the wild is certainly also due to the impression these big cats make on visitors to zoos, if they are kept well, according to modern methods. A lot of money has been donated for saving tigers; incomparably more than for lions. Not only is breeding tigers in zoos not a problem, it has actually become a problem because these big cats reproduce so well: there are too many offspring. But if the demand for 'tiger products' remains high on East Asian markets, the pressure on tigers living in the wild due to poaching will not flag. After all, it was and still is poaching that has decimated the last stocks of tigers in the wild in India and East Siberia to such an extent that even in some nature reserves, we are concerned about the last tigers' survival. Several isolated incidences which had even been individual races of tiger are extinct. It is significant to note that it was not conflicts with the local population in the areas where tigers live that had led to the diminishing incidences of tigers, but the high black-market prices for traditional tiger products in the Far East. If China can use products from tigers raised for this purpose to meet this demand, which will surely diminish as the country modernizes, the pressure on the populations in the wild will ease, and the odds that this highly impressive big cat will survive will

increase. Observing tigers in the Indian reserves of Rantham-
bore, Sariska, and Khana as well as in Nepal's Chitwan National
Park, renowned for their outstanding quality, ranks among the
greatest experiences nature tourists can enjoy. Tiger safaris will
continue to secure the survival of the animal, even on the Indian
subcontinent, populated so densely by humans.

The large animals that are more difficult to observe as well as
those which can be experienced in national parks with spectacular landscapes are faring better than they did even half a century
ago. They have the restrictions of the Convention on International Trade in Endangered Species of Wild Fauna and Flora
(CITES) to thank for their comeback. When this convention was
followed by a comprehensive ban on trade in species such as the
leopard (*Panthera pardus*), the ocelot (*Felis pardalis*), the jaguar
(*Panthera onca*), and other spotted cats, their furs became practically worthless, because the ban applied to them as so-called
Appendix I species. Accordingly, their stocks recovered, or at
least, their decline was slowed. All of a sudden, it was no longer
chic to wrap oneself in a leopard coat to demonstrate wealth
and fame. On the contrary – women who wore such furs had to
reckon with verbal attacks and public contempt. The leopard,
the most flexible of these spotted cats, responded best. Its stocks
increased, especially in Africa. For years, the chance to observe
leopards on a photo safari has no longer been a particular stroke
of luck.

The South American spotted cats are not faring as well
because their stocks were much smaller than those of their
African and South Asian relatives to begin with. South America's
jungles provide incomparably less food in the form of animals
of the appropriate size than the animal-rich forests, savannahs,
and steppes of Africa. When the Europeans introduced grazing
cattle, they brought in new prey that was more abundant and

easier especially for jaguars, but also for pumas, to hunt. With dire consequences for the predatory big cats. Even in the US, one of the richest countries of the world, it is difficult to preserve the puma (*Felis concolor*) because the farmers are not prepared to accept the losses of productive livestock. A nature reserve rich enough in natural prey and big enough to ensure survival of an incidence of pumas or jaguars has to be more than ten times the size of a corresponding reserve for lions, leopards and the like in Africa.

Particularly in South America, the challenge will be to compensate for the losses in livestock by safari tourism for observing jaguars, pumas, and ocelots, with numbers of tourists comparable to those in Africa and South Asia. We can count on this approach being successful where such tourism takes place or where the methods employed on large farms are designed to deal with this problem from the outset. The wild animal farms of South Africa and Namibia have proven this to be true. They provide secure private reserves for predators such as the cheetah (*Acinonyx jubatus*) which have become extremely rare, and the prospects at least for the near future do not look at all bad there.

There is similarly positive news regarding the development of stocks of elephants. The ban on trading ivory within the framework of CITES has not entirely stopped poaching, but it has forced it back to such an extent that the stocks began to grow back. Today, the trade in ivory, which has been legalized in part, is not even the core of the elephant problem, but the overuse of the nature reserves caused by the animals themselves. The numbers of elephants have simply become too large in some places. Entire herds had to be killed off to prevent the elephants from destroying their own habitat. Wherever these largest of the land animals exist, they inevitably change the habitat, and the reason for this is not only because they remain more or less confined in the reserves as they can no longer migrate unimpeded across greater distances as they did before. It is elephants', buffalos', and all the other large animals' nature to profoundly change their habitats. The animals' grazing and the fact that they kept any trees short facilitated the development and preservation of savannahs where woods could have flourished quite well. Not just mankind, but other large mammals s well, change their habitats by using them.

Problems with increasing incidence of the animals are the best proof for the effectiveness of protective measures. This applies at the global scale as well as the regional and local scales. If we compare conditions in Central Europe with the few examples of global species preservation, we will see that the results are much better, not merely comparable. In a nutshell: there are more larger and large mammals as well as large birds in Central Europe today than 100 years ago; stocks of some species are greater than they have ever been since mankind created a cultural landscape. In Central Europe, this finding concerns red deer (*Cervus elaphus*), fallow deer (*Dama dama*), roe deer (*Capreolus capreolus*), moose (*Alces alces*), and wild boars (*Sus scrofa*), which live in the wild, as well as two deer species that occur only locally. The size of the deer population has attained a level that it has probably never reached since its return after the end of the last ice age in Central Europe. The reason for this success and also for that of the red deer are comprehensive measures on the part of hunters to tend the animals. Over the last twenty-five to thirty years, the population of wild boars has jumped by a factor of ten in some places such as Bavaria, in spite of all attempts to regulate their numbers. The spreading of elks (moose) to Central Europe that is under way, after their establishing a stable population in Lower Austria, is by no means the new major danger to road traffic, considering the masses of large wild boars and their short legs. A collision with a large wild boar is more likely to cause a severe accident than a collision with a long-legged elk. But even the publicly uttered deliberations on the part of ministries and the press when controversially debating the spread of elks express that the problem is not that the cultural landscaped could not sustain elks, but that the concerns are about road traffic safety and possible game bite to young trees potentially caused by elks. In Scandinavia, the animal depicted on traffic signs warning of wild animals is the elk, not the small deer, as in Europe. But predators, too, have survived and are spreading, not only the herbivores that are 'peaceful' by nature. Wolves are currently approaching Central Europe from the northeast, as they did in the centuries of the Little Ice Age with its terrible winters. Wolves survived in Spain, in Italy where they advanced to the outskirts of Rome, and in the countries of Central Eastern Europe which now belong to the European Union. Today, in 2009, wolves have already reproduced successfully in Brandenburg, Germany. They are again part of the fauna, even if their numbers are still very small. The odds for the return of the Eurasian lynx (*Lynx lynx*) are not as bad as was assumed a good thirty years ago when its reintroduction was initiated. Even though they are still brought down here and there, their prospects for the future have been improving since they have been able to migrate from the east. There is certainly plenty of food for the Eurasian lynx in the form of the Central European deer population. Where losses of sheep have to be expected, it is important to put appropriate measures to counteract and compensate for them in place in due time. Such measures were lacking when a brown bear from the Lake Garda region (Brenta) migrated from Northern Italy to Bavaria in the early summer of 2006. The bear, named Bruno by the media, was shot by order of the authorities for being a 'problem bear.' Regardless of the true problems connected with the killed sheep and the mere appearance of a brown bear in a region where there had been no bears for two whole human generations, the reactions of the population express the sympathies which even such large animals enjoy today. The question was correctly raised whether it is in order that a species such as the brown bear, which enjoys priority protection in all of Europe, is protected in the mountains of the Tatra and the Carpathians, but not in Germany, and that the millions of euros raised in Germany are used to preserve bears on Kamchatka in the Far East, but that financial compensation for the relatively small damages in Germany is not sufficient to secure the bear's survival.

The debate about damages is by now affecting the greatest success story in species preservation in Central Europe and far beyond, namely the reintroduction of the European beaver (*Castor fiber*). Heavier on average than a roe deer when fully grown, the largest rodent in the entire northern hemisphere had been completely exterminated in the eighteenth and nineteenth centuries, with the exception of a few small remaining populations. In Europe, they remained in existence in inaccessible parts of the southern border region between Norway and Sweden, along the Elbe River between Dessau and Magdeburg in Germany, and along the lower Rhône in France. In the early twentieth century, these remaining populations had also become so small that one had to expect the species' extinction. Possibly encouraged by the massive promotion on the part of the fur industry in Russia and in the still-young Soviet Union, which even introduced North American beavers and muskrats, Sweden began to reintroduce European beavers from southern Norway. The incidence of Rhône beavers still remained unnoticed for a longer period. It could sustain itself, as could the population along the Elbe River. The Elbe beavers had to cope with the catastrophic pollution of the Elbe and its tributary, the Mulde

River. They managed, and slowly began to spread again. East Germany supported them by local redistribution into adjacent river systems. In the mean time, Finland, too, had reintroduced beavers. In Bavaria, the Bavarian Union for Nature Conservation, headed by Hubert Weinzierl, developed the first ideas to reintroduce the animal. The project was started in 1970 with beavers from Sweden, and was continued for a full decade. In Austria as well, beavers were reintroduced along the Danube and Salzach Rivers at the same time. The Inn River, whose lower course forms the border between Austria and Germany, became the center of reintroduction in the northern region of the foothills of the Alps. A second center was established on the upper course of the Danube. Soon, other German federal states followed suit. Towards the end of the twentieth century, it was entirely clear that the reintroduction had succeeded. Currently, beavers occur in almost the places where they had formerly lived along rivers and larger streams. The population in Bavaria has practically followed the ideal development that is to be expected if there are no serious losses or setbacks (Figure 13).

On the one hand, the development of the beaver population in Bavaria shows how long it takes to establish a new population that can sustain itself independently and continue to reproduce. Only after about twenty years was it certain that the beaver had made it. And in this case, the general public had been very sympathetic to the animals' reintroduction, and there had been no resistance worth mentioning. On the other hand, the beaver's comeback can also be considered proof for the fact that the living conditions in our cultural landscape have by no means become fundamentally inimical to nature. It has already been pointed out that a beaver family has settled even in Munich, on the Isar River near the Deutsches Museum. Losses due to road traffic, even if they do occur when beavers roam the land seeking new

Population development of the beaver *Castor fiber* in Bavaria

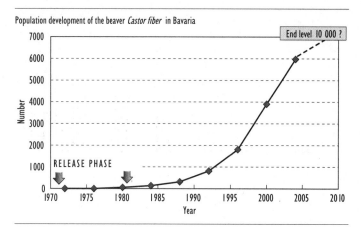

Figure 13 Progress of the reintroduction of the beaver in Bavaria. At close to 10 000 individuals, the population is approaching the presumed capacity of Bavaria's available beaver habitat

waters, were not a significant impediment to the beaver population spreading.

Birds, especially large birds, doubtless have it better in this regard. Astounding successes can be recorded for them in Central Europe, densely populated and intensively used as it is. In sum, the incidence of the most large bird species has increased in the last quarter-century, but some species have increased in particular, and with global significance. Above all, two birds of prey bound to bodies of water must be mentioned: the white-tailed sea eagle (*Haliaaetus albicilla*) and the osprey (*Pandion haliaetus*). They survived the Europe-wide, partly even world-wide decline of their populations on the East German lakes, not least thanks to very effective protection of the species during East German times. In the 1970s, the population gradually began to

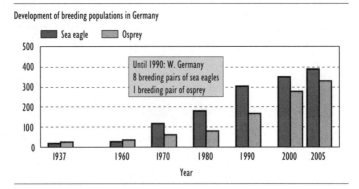

Development of breeding populations in Germany

Figure 14 Development of the breeding populations of the sea eagle and osprey in Germany

The sea eagle population in Eastern Germany makes up around ten percent of the total population of this species in Europe

grow, and this has continued to the present day and has spread to the birds settling in new places outside the area of the former East Germany. Since the beginning of the twenty-first century, East Germany has belonged to the regions with the densest population of these two large birds of prey in the world. Both species have built up populations (Figure 14) that are 'on the safe side', with more than 500 breeding pairs each now (2009), and can contribute to both species spreading further.

Individual pairs of the white-tailed sea eagle and the osprey are currently brooding even in northern Bavaria. They occur in other places in Europe as well, in growing numbers, with just under 10,000 breeding pairs of the osprey and roughly 4,000 of the white-tailed sea eagle, so their future viability is secured, as is that of the eagle of the high mountains, the golden eagle (*Aquila chrysaetos*), in the Alps. For years, all available areas have been 'covered' by golden eagle territories. The days of the almost complete annihilation of the eagle have been overcome. Even the bearded vulture (*Gypaetus barbatus*), which is larger yet, was successfully reintroduced to the Alps – for centuries, the bird had wrongly suffered a bad reputation as a 'lammergeier,' i.e., a vulture that kills lambs.

Europe has been experiencing strong increases in the numbers of white egret, in particular great white egret (*Egretta alba*). In some parts of southern Germany, more of these impressive herons can be found in the winter than gray herons (*Ardea cinerea*), which breed there in large numbers, but are decimated time and again. The little egrets (*Egretta garzetta*) have succeeded in breeding north of the Alps. If these dapper birds are not begrudged the fish they must live on, then they will have a future in Germany. The birds' decorative feathers, highly sought-after for fashionable ladies' hats in the late nineteenth century, had become their downfall.

The populations of the greater (European) flamingo (*Phoenicopteros ruber*) are increasing in the Mediterranean region. From the southeast, from the gorges of the Balkans, the black stork (*Ciconia nigra*), which had become extremely rare, has spread again and its numbers are about to surpass those of the much better-known white stork (*Ciconia ciconia*). Slowly but surely, its previous skittishness is on the wane. The great cormorant (*Phalacrocorax carbo*) has become so ubiquitous that the freshwater fishing industry is forming a common front against the bird and demanding its decimation. The incidences of many other species have increased as well, and this statement holds for practically all species of birds of prey. Their persecution continues only in exceptional cases. Major cities have become secure islands for some of their species. Enormous flocks of wild geese come to spend the winter in the areas of northwestern Germany where winters are mild. In southern Germany, new and growing populations of graylag geese (*Anser anser*) have developed. They can be seen flying around over Munich during the migration season, presumably because of their instinct to migrate. Nonetheless, they cannot leave the city, even though a system of aquatic bird reserves could lure them away; that system of reserves has been functioning better and better, and the aquatic birds are not hunted there, as they are near the reservoirs on the lower course of the Inn River. Graylag goose populations have developed near the places where the return of the most special bird of the European world of birds, the waldrapp (hermit ibis, *Geronticus eremita*), an ibis measuring seventy to eighty centimeters, is to be enabled. In the Middle Ages and the early modern era, the waldrapp lived in town walls and castles, for instance in Salzburg and on Burghausen Castle, which is today one of the reintroduction centers. The bird is almost completely extinct in the wild. A single incidence which provides a few offspring in Morocco still remains, as well as two more with uncertain futures in eastern Turkey and northern Syria. The waldrapp survived in zoos and bird parks, and the birds that are now being returned to the wild stem from such breeding. Since they have to learn to find their way to appropriate winter quarters, they are trained with ultra-light airplanes so that they can find the proper (and safe) route. This is a gargantuan effort. Without the personal and emotionally deeply-rooted commitment of those involved in the waldrapp project, the enterprise would surely fail. Such commitment does exist. It points to the reasons and motives that move people to protect nature.

Why Protection?

Mankind is faced with major problems. That is not much different today from the situation in earlier times when daily life was fraught with risk. Many people today, especially the well-off, view the future more grimly than they did just a few decades ago. But in addition to these one billion people who are relatively well-off, there are also five, soon six billion people who have to think more about today than about tomorrow because many of them are struggling to survive. It may seem like a luxury: the rich can afford to rhapsodize about beautiful butterflies on meadows dotted with flowers and travel to New Guinea to gaze in amazement at birds of paradise in courtship in the wild, while at the same time, so many people go hungry. A simple comparison, which admittedly does have its weaknesses, may make clear what this is about. It is about a rich country such as Germany in the middle of Europe, which is well-off by global standards. Cities, at least if they are large enough, afford the expense of a zoo. Out in the country, livestock live in barns or out in the fields. Plants and animals must yield a profit there. In the city, they can be a source of joy or amusement. Modern zoos developed out of the old menageries whose roots were ultimately in the much older circuses where people, trained wrestlers, took on the beasts. Mostly, if not every time, the human won, and this is still the case in bullfighting, which is about life and death.

In the European Middle Ages, the closed garden, the *Hortus conclusus*, was the venue where people tended tamed and cultivated nature, and where the aristocracy could delight in it. Animals as well as plants, even those cultivated for their beautiful flowers, were merely there to serve a purpose. Those are the roots of the legal stance that animals are 'objects,' and not, for example, living creatures related more or less closely to human beings. That, however, is how Hinduism feels about them, and this is roughly how the Buddhist concept of nature considers all living things. In contrast, they were to be removed from the cultivated nature of the Western world, just like the plants which were weeded because they caused damage. This stance is set down in the Bible and many other religious writings, and has become Western cultures' outlook on life. Humans are outside of nature, and nature is supposed to either serve them, whatever purposes they may define for nature, or be cultivated in order to become civilized and worthy of human beings. The three great Western religions agree for the most part in this regard. Their attitude is summed up in the biblical command, 'Be fruitful, and multiply, and replenish the earth, and subdue it." Only in rare or exceptional cases did a caring or, as we would call it today, 'sustainable' form of use come about, because nature was considered to be a free good, and animals and plants remained rated as 'objects.' In the West, great research efforts on the genetic makeup of organisms have been necessary in recent years to deduce and prove the unity of all living things – emphasized in the great Eastern religions and philosophies – scientifically; the field of molecular genetics, which emerged from such research, has contributed as well.

Nonetheless, some Christians still have difficulties accepting the unity of life. Some groups categorically refuse the concept that biological diversity has developed because of evolution. Therefore, the more forcefully the concept of humankind's special status is advocated, the stronger the polarization of mankind and nature. Where, in apparently primitive, animistic ways, people have considered themselves to be part of nature and partners of nature, even partners of the game they hunt to survive, lively diversity has continued to exist. Where Hindu, Buddhist, or similar philosophies of life not only considered mankind part of the general stream of life, but also emphasized humans' connections with nature and duties towards it – in spite of their distinctive features, or even precisely because of them – humans and animals were more successful at living with one another. Even if hunger afflicted people or caused them to die in great numbers, this fundamental esteem of other living creatures remained.

Anyone who has experienced how the poorest of the poor in India scavenge for remnants of edible food in garbage dumps, and then share their meager and putrid findings with a dog, all skin and bones that itself has been foraging around, will be touched more deeply and in a different way by this kind of relationship between humans and animals than by peering a whale in the eye or by experiencing how a seal is born in the midst of a group of people. At the other end of the spectrum in their relationship with nature are people who deliberately kill or torture animals even though they do not have to live on them and have not been harmed by them in any way. This group of people is characterized by carelessness and lack of knowledge of the consequences of their actions, combined with all-too-egoistic interest in their own goals. For them, nature is merely a means to an end – their own ends, of course. In order to reach them (and rake in the profits), they often use the public interest as a pretense, without being commissioned by the public to do so. More than two thousand years ago, when someone presented a project, the Romans would ask for good reason to whose advantage it would be.

This question about the distribution of benefits, therefore, is the core of the problem regarding the protection of species or natural areas, whether or not it is expressed directly. Who will benefit if previous uses cannot be continued? Who will lose? Who stands to gain? And why should one group benefit while another has to face losses?

Nature protection usually employs a three-tiered line of argument. The first tier is the principle of (direct) benefit. The rationale is egocentric. "Since I/we (want to) enjoy benefits, you must take a back seat or accept the negative impacts." The second form uses the approach of societal responsibility. It denounces egoism and counters it with altruism, the benefits for the community. "Everyone benefits if a few have to deal with the drawbacks." One could also call this line of reasoning 'sociocentric'; not necessarily social, because the benefit for the general public may potentially remain very theoretical. Often, many members of the so-called general public are not interested in the project in question at all. The third tier assumes the largest possible community, the diversity of life as a whole. Representatives of this school of thought argue that we do not have the right to exterminate other living creatures, and that individual people in particular must not do so. After all, the life forms belong to the common stream of life on earth and/or to divine creation, 'as we do.' Nobody may presume the right to pass judgment on the value of other living things. In Hinduism, this attitude is surely most strongly pronounced, but some streams of Western nature protection and the so called deep ecology movement represent this biocentric worldview. The Earth, called Gaia, is considered to be a holistic organism. From such a lofty perspective, some people are extremely pessimistic about mankind and regard it as the most detrimental species and the greatest 'mistake of evolution.' As a species, humanity will exterminate itself, or will at least (have to) make way for purified human beings in a better future. From this perspective, species protection can be justified as a necessity for the 'time thereafter,' when the Earth will have liberated itself from the cancerous growth of mankind. The surviving species can then proceed into a happier future.

In a concrete case, when the debate is about particular species, fairly different lines of argument for their protection emerge. For example, one or more species are to be preserved because they are useful or could become useful at some future point. This argument of utility is very popular, because it includes in its justification the current lack of knowledge that could (soon) be replaced by better knowledge. In other words, it would be short-sighted to exterminate a species now if it could be useful in the future. This reason is advanced frequently for plants and inconspicuous small animals because it is practically the only way to convey the idea why this unimpressive plant or that small bug should not die out even though it is obvious that there are many other similar ones. One advantage of the reasoning using potential utility is that all useful plants and a large part of the species that are used in natural medicine were originally inconspicuous and could only become as valuable they are now because their benefits were studied in detail. This argument cannot be applied so easily for useful animals because their qualities were apparent enough even before they were domesticated. But a much larger number of animals gained immense importance as pets that are kept in bird cages, terrariums, and aquariums, although they do not provide direct utility.

Pets are a billion-dollar business. Nobody could have predicted that an inconspicuous small greenish-yellow finch native to the Canary Islands, the Canary bird (*Serinus canaria*), would some day become one of the most popular and common cage birds in the form of the cultured canary. The same applies to the budgerigar (*Melopsittacus undulatus*). When the British discovered the wild bird flying around Australia in the millions, they asked the aborigines what they called it. Their response sounded like 'budgerigar,' which is still the British term for it, even though what the aborigines said meant only that these birds taste good ('good to eat'). The golden hamster (*Mesocricetus auratus*) has a similarly wondrous story: the many millions of hamsters, bred in the most diverse forms, are said to be the descendents of a single female of this small Syrian hamster species. It had been caught in 1938. The population in the wild either became extinct long ago or has become extremely rare.

The discovery of medicinal properties was almost coincidental for numerous plants whose value was recognized and exploited due to their pharmaceutical effectiveness. For instance, an apparently inconspicuous periwinkle from Madagascar and a North American yew species supply substances that are effective against certain forms of cancer. Quinine, made from the rind of the cinchona tree that grows scattered in the Amazon forests and has no relevance as timber, is one of the best-known active ingredients from natural sources. It was the first anti-malarial remedy; however, more effective ones have been developed in recent decades. A similarly inconspicuous tree species from the Amazon region, *Hevea brasiliensis*, the rubber tree par excellence, became world-famous in a different way. It is not one of the numerous species which are called rubber trees because their milk-like sap contains a liquid similar to latex, but rather the type of natural rubber that was instrumental for the success of motorized automobiles. Without rubber tires filled with air, the development of the automobile would certainly not have taken place so quickly, and it might have taken a different course altogether. The success of natural rubber was so great that during the rubber boom in the Amazon region, the town of Manaus, completely surrounded by inaccessible rain forests, boasted a world-class opera house. That region's rubber boom collapsed when smugglers had succeeded in spiriting the tree's seeds out of the country and using them to establish rubber plantations in Southeast Asia. The theft of the *Hevea brasiliensis* seeds is the archetypal example for why countries with high natural species-richness have to take precautions against their treasures being stolen, causing them to lose out on the profits to be made.

(Central) European flora also offers many examples of medicinal plants. The beautifully flowering foxglove plants (species of *Digitalis*) are the source of the glycoside used widely in modern

medicine to treat heart disease. A remedy for reducing blood clot-
ting, thus preventing strokes, is extracted from the well-known
medicinal leech. For centuries, people used plants as medicines
before modern chemistry was able to partially replace them or
make them more effective. Thus, the line of reasoning based on
species' potential utility is on solid footing. The fact that this alone
is not enough is often due to the conditions on the ground. If the
local population is very poor, it will be difficult to convince people
to protect a small rodent that could be eaten or that damages the
meager supplies of food because one day, it might turn into a
second golden hamster story. Cultivating useful plants for food
will certainly be given priority over medicinal plants, especially if
they have not yet been discovered, but are only presumed to have
such properties. In a 'hand-to-mouth' situation, the rare small
fish will not end up in a scientist's aquarium, but on people's
plates. And where wolves cause great damage to the reindeer or
sheep that nomadic herders depend on, people will combat them
and strive to annihilate them. Such conditions, which are by no
means uncommon, make it more difficult for the equally common
line of reasoning that the species in question must be protected,
and damage they cause must be accepted in the interest of the
whole of society, usually the interest of the state. Where societal
inequality is severe, it is only all too understandable that the poor
population that cannot afford meat from slaughterhouses will
capture wild animals with slings and traps, even if they are offi-
cially banned. We in Germany gave a textbook example of such
behavior in the case of 'Bruno', the bear in the summer of 2006,
even though nobody could claim that the property they needed
for survival was threatened by this immigrant bear. Even though
recreational fishermen's livelihoods do not depend on their catch,
they do not want to accept alleged or actual damages to the fish
populations due to birds that must live on the fish.

Time and again, the experiences in rich countries demonstrate that it is precisely those people who could actually afford them who are not prepared to accept even minimal losses, even if the general public has great interest in protecting the animals in question. Pointing to the common good does not work where 'others' benefit. People demand compensation at the very least. The demand for compensation tends to be greater the richer the population in question is, because wealthier people calculate damage in different ways from the poor.

Outside of elite circles and the population of major cities, where 'biocentrism' is developing to gushing 'biophilia,' the urgent admonition that all living creatures are part of the natural whole and that nothing must be taken from it is practically ineffective. Edward O. Wilson, the pioneer and forward thinker of the global movement to preserve biodiversity, did not intend for biophilia to be understood in this way. Moreover, pondering our natural origins and marveling at nature's diversity enable us to adopt a more ethical attitude towards it. Such an ethical stance is surely highly honorable and would deserve to be integrated centrally in Judaism, Christianity, and Islam. But it will not be particularly helpful in those other parts of the planet plagued by poverty and illnesses, by abysmal social conditions and political repression.

In the end, then, the reasoning for species protection remains what has always been successful everywhere, namely egoism restricted and guided by the society in question. In the rich countries which can afford so much, and so much which is unnecessary, appeals to ethics and to higher social responsibility for the community at large may well result in certain successes. The fact that some nature protection goals have been incorporated into laws and regulations proves this both in a fundamental and a limited way. After all, the alleged or actual necessities were, as a rule, watered down a lot when put in legally binding form, thereby making them more or less ineffective. The (ethical) duty may have been fulfilled in a formal manner, but in reality, almost nothing changed. As explained above, the German Federal Nature Protection Act and the nature protection acts of the federal states elaborated within the framework it provides limit nature lovers most of all, but the direct users of nature least. Where, on the other hand, egoism is plainly visible and taken for granted, rather than being concealed in the background, as in hunting law, the Hunting Acts do not encumber the hunters most of all; instead, their interests are supposed to be promoted as well as possible. The framework and the limits it imposes do regulate personal interests in such laws considerably, but in principle, the priority they are given remains in place.

Under such societal conditions, nature protection must inevitably develop into a different form of using nature because the many egoistic goals of millions of people can be pushed through with regard to other parts of society if they are bundled together, rather than by attempting to employ only idealistic ideas and reasons based on points in time far in the future. For these reasons, too, we must renew and reinforce our demand for the creation of private nature reserves by non-state nature protection organizations. In this way, reconciling interests with the previous users of nature can by all means benefit many people, including future generations, altruistically. The fact that the goal is primarily to help animals and plants is then shifted to become an internal reason for the organizations in question, one which can be measured by its successes (for nature and the people interested in it) from the outside.

At the international or global level, this approach would not work, of course, at least not as directly. Here, the rich countries and their populations must continue to provide monetary compensation for the poorer and poor countries to preserve their natural treasures. Whatever cannot be achieved sufficiently by direct nature tourism should be compensated for by other means. Development aid is a possibility, as is debt relief. In both cases, however, appropriate safeguards and obligations must be built in so that the funds are supplied and the debts cancelled only if there are sufficient guarantees for sustaining the protected areas or species. Only if these species have a real value, not a fictitious one, a value significantly higher than any other use, will there be prospects for success. The old, widespread system of simply declaring certain areas or creatures taboo does not work any more in the modern world. All in all, nature protection will have to demand that the tried and tested principle of tit for tat be applied to nature protection, as has long been customary in the business world.

In any case, however, the very diverse conditions in different parts of the globe must be taken into account comprehensively. A line of argument which may be convincing in the rich Western world may be entirely inappropriate elsewhere. The justification that fits the local situation best will always be the one that will be understood and possibly accepted. The cultures of the world differ from one another. In the interest of human diversity, too, they will continue to be different for a long time, and will bring forth new forms of cultural life time and again. 'Nature is a cultural endeavor," are the words Hubert Markl, longtime President of the German Research Foundation and the Max Planck Society chose so aptly. How much nature, and how much of its nature a culture protects will also become a criterion of that culture's quality. Nature is an endeavor for providing for the future. What kind of future can nature have, with mankind continuing to grow?

A Future for Biodiversity – or No Future?

The human population will continue to grow, but we cannot predict with certainty how many people will live on earth in 100 years or more. What is certain, however, is that the number of people going hungry will increase quite substantially before population growth comes to a halt and begins to decrease in major regions outside of Europe, too. This will result in pressure on nature in two ways. The human world will expand and take up more space, and food production must be increased. For nature, this means that even more land than today will be cultivated in order to exhaust the 'last reserves.' In any case, hardly any good, productive land is left that has not yet been utilized. If less-productive land is used, the areas under cultivation must accordingly be larger. The amount of grain that grows on a square kilometer in Central Europe or North America will then need a larger area to grow, in extreme cases, ten times as much land, or even more.

That is the proportion for cattle grazing, for example. The best English pastureland yields (and can carry) up to twenty metric tons of cattle per square kilometer. Poor tropical grazing land can nourish at most one-tenth of that amount. The more unfavorable the conditions of production become, the lower the yield – but usually, the greater the biodiversity that exists there. The luxuriant tropical rain forests of Amazonia offer so little for small deer species, comparable to European deer, that the same number of animals shot per year – roughly a million – practically led to their extinction there, while in Europe, it has kept their populations highly productive. Almost without exception, the successes of CITES, the Convention on International Trade in Endangered Species of Wild Fauna and Flora, concern species of animals that live under difficult circumstances with low yields. Persecution by hunting or other means brought them almost to extinction. When this persecution was stopped because CITES prohibits trade and traffic with animals of these species and products of these animals, their populations increased again. As we demonstrated using the example of the leopard in Africa: the better the living conditions are, the faster the populations have grown. In contrast to the leopard, the jaguar is hardly recovering because its habitats are continuing to dwindle due to forest clearing, and the illegal takings are not declining for the reasons mentioned above. On the other hand, it is precisely the large mammals and large birds in Europe, which used to be hunted more or less intensely, but that now enjoy comprehensive protection, which are spreading so strongly that there is reason to hope that almost the entire spectrum of species will success-fully return, and to most of the areas they previously inhabited. Should we even dare to make predictions about the future of biodiversity, given that the circumstances are incomparably more complicated in the individual local situations?

Perhaps we should not dare to forecast, but to hope. For example, many countries of the world have fairly good laws governing the preservation of nature, in particular also the pro-tection of biodiversity. Nature protection laws exist in the vast majority of countries. The most impressive successes in Europe have been achieved where regulations, which are binding just as national laws in the Member States are, have effected compre-hensive protection of the world of birds (with the exception of a group of species which are subject to hunting law).

The European Birds Directive is one such regulation for species protection. It was expanded and tightened in the so-called Habitats Directive (the Council Directive on the Conser-vation of natural habitats and of wild fauna and flora), which protects, in other words, the worlds of animals and plants and the special places where they live (habitats). But in Russia, India,

Africa, South America and Australia, as well as in South East Asia, numerous good reserves and effective protective regulations exist. Papua-New Guinea and Indonesia (including the western part of the island of New Guinea called Irian Jaya) protects the birds of paradise and the spectacular birdwings (Ornithoptera) which are among the most beautiful and rarest butterflies in the world. The achievements of poor African countries – not least their national parks – to protect their large animals, which are by no means always harmless, by far surpasses the accomplishments of Germany and other European countries in this respect. In our part of the world, small insects that hardly anyone knows and that cannot be preserved without protecting their habitats as well, are granted protection. The species listed in the CITES appendices are monitored at regular intervals to ascertain whether new species must be included in strict protection or others can be 'downgraded' and partly removed from the list thanks to the positive effects of protection. In this way, species protection is moving towards being a balancing process on a fundamentally rational basis which determines what is necessary and makes it possible to reward successes. In the final analysis, it is not all that important whether we are considering small birds which bird lovers can keep as pets in cages or aviaries, birds of prey with high symbolic status value (large falcons with which one can practice falconry), or crocodiles bred on farms because sought-after crocodile leather is made from their skins. What is important is that the status of species is determined accurately enough in their natural incidences and the population trends continue to be identified. Then, it is possible to intervene in a meaningful way, or restrictions can be relaxed.

The work of nature protection organizations such as the **IUCN** (International Union for the Conservation of Nature and Natural Resources), the **WWF** (World Wide Fund for Nature),

Conservation International, the Frankfurt Zoological Society and many others has been very effective for decades. Their achievements demonstrate that nature protection is by no means only a societal movement in rich countries, but has long become a global concern. This alone gives us grounds for hope and for cautious optimism. Another reason has already been mentioned. The areas most important for preserving biodiversity are located more on the margins and in countries that do not necessarily need these spaces for their own populations. In particular the South American countries have such large reserves of land that securing the core areas of biodiversity in the American tropics does not compromise their land use significantly. Fundamentally similar circumstances are to be found almost all over the world. People have either always avoided such areas, or have hardly settled there at all.

In the tropical countries and in subtropical areas and regions on the edges of the tropics, a different process has been under way for decades which has been lessening the pressure on the centers of biodiversity over time. People are moving to the cities, which are growing much more quickly than the rural population. As problematic as this process of urbanization and the social consequences it entails may be, they do relieve the pressure on some rural areas. Soon, more than half of humankind will live in major cities and megacities. In other words, by no means does the growing human population imply the end of biological diversity. We certainly have room to maneuver, to take the necessary steps, if international nature protection focuses on the centers of biodiversity.

What, then, is to be done? Recommendations abound. Few of them are realistic because other necessities or overly powerful opponents stand in the way of their becoming reality. The largest players, such as the World Bank with its lending, the European

Union with its agricultural policy, and the growing giants China and India with their resource use, will continue to have the largest impacts on the loss of biodiversity. But the poor countries, too, have become a major factor in global development due to the overexploitation of nature they are more or less forced to engage in. It is imperative to link loans or development aid to clear, verifiable guidelines for dealing with nature. Nature must no longer be considered a freely available good that can be utilized and used up at will. Preserving nature must become part of a global partnership. Assigning value to nature is not enough in and of itself. Partnership means more. It must also be founded on values and appreciation, and must be able to rely on them. This requirement is also directed towards us. We must not continue to grant ourselves a clean conscience for shifting the exploitation of nature to the Third World or the threshold countries because it is cheaper for us to do so.

A good criterion are the advantages and disadvantages of particular locations which have been taken into account in the business world for a long time. Under given circumstances (as against changing them laboriously), those things are to be produced which turn out best there. The diversity of the earth then expresses itself in differing qualities, especially in the qualities of nature, or biodiversity. Tourism, in particular nature tourism, recognized this long ago and has focused its goals towards it. As with all good things, or things meant well, however, eco-tourism can also have destructive effects. That does not make it expendable, because a lack of eco-tourism would leave even more room for the destruction of nature. But the more the millions upon millions of tourists assert that they come because quality standards are maintained in the utilization of nature at the destination in question, too, the more it will be possible to enforce those standards. In this way, every single one of us can make a contribution – not (just) with money, but with the demands we make. Just as we value good, wholesome food, we should appreciate well-preserved nature highly. Taking action in time against all-too-destructive projects is one of the core concerns of the nature protection organizations. Making every endeavor to support them, especially when they prove their seriousness by means of the verifiability of their projects and successes, is a mandate of our times. This applies at the international level as well as at the national and regional ones. Making intense commitments of time and finances for nature protection certainly deserves appreciation similar to that for social ends. And everyone who can realize the beautiful principle of 'live and let live' in their own gardens or on their own land should do so. A billion Indians afford this 'let live' under conditions incomparably more difficult than ours in our European-American civilization.

Hence, nature protection will continue to be an emotional affair, and probably to an increasing extent. Currently, the negative predominates in nature protection. It must urgently be balanced by the positive. If we continue to announce losses and catastrophes and spread an atmosphere of doom, nature protection as a concern will not have a future. Biodiversity, on the other hand, will have a future, and it will be possible to save most of if, if we give it new significance. We must make its preservation a cultural achievement.

It will never be possible to determine how many species of animals and plants the earth 'needs.' But nobody can state which species are expendable, either. And we can be held to account for what we could have preserved.

Glossary

Ideally, technical terms should be both precise and comprehensible. Meeting these demands, however, is impossible for two reasons. First, the great diversity of nature, especially living nature, is not easily accommodated by the categories of our thinking and language, and therefore resists demarcation and definition. After all, no definition comes without weaknesses and exceptions. Additionally, there is often marked divergence in views as to how a particular term should be applied. Many scientists would disagree, for example, with the currently popular use of 'forest ecosystem' to designate an individual, specific forest. This must be borne in mind with respect to all of the following explanations of technical terms from this book.

Second, scientific terms often cannot be fittingly translated into a generally understandable language, as even the explanation of what they mean assumes more or less extensive prior knowledge. Considerable simplification is required in explaining many terms. For this reason, the natural sciences use technical terms based in Latin and Classical Greek. This practice also prevents the confusion that could arise if a scientific term matched a word in the common language. Direct translations of technical terms into modern vernacular would yield highly curious expressions. For instance, the corresponding expression for 'biocenosis' (a community of animals and plants in nature) would be 'living banquet.'

For these reasons, the explanations provided in this glossary are not intended and should not be thought of as scientific definitions, but as aids to understanding. It is unavoidable that significant differences arise in the meaning of certain terms as applied in various books in this series. The use of 'biosphere' here as compared with M. Latif's explanation of the word in *Climate Change: The Point of no Return* is but one example.

abiotic – referring to nonliving nature

biocenosis – a group of species that jointly, and therefore somewhat interdependently, inhabit a certain area (biotope). The fauna of a section of a forest forms a biocenosis, as does the teeming, if almost invisible, life in a sample of garden soil.

biodiversity – the total variety of living things (species), their internal (genetic) diversity, and the biotopes formed by living things. Biodiversity is thus more comprehensive than variety of species.

biome – a broad habitat of the earth such as the boreal forest (taiga) or the Mediterranean sclerophyll ('hard-leaved') woodland region. Biomes overlay the continents in zones or belts as determined by general climatic conditions. Their boundaries are not sharply drawn, but formed by more or less gradual transition zones between them, depending on the geographic situation.

biosphere – the part of the earth which is inhabited by living organisms, taking in both its surface and part of its crust. It stretches over the earth's inanimate geosphere like a living skin. Life exists from the polar ice masses and highest mountain peaks down to the deepest depths of the oceans and into the rock of the earth's upper crust. The oceans and the surface of the land constitute the greatest part of the biosphere.

biotic – referring to living processes in nature caused or sustained by life activities

biotope – 'place of life'; site or space in which various species live. Currently, the term is applied especially to near-natural habitats such as marshes, ponds, alluvial forests, dry grasslands, etc. More fundamentally, however, anything in which living organisms are found constitutes a biotope. In reference to a particular species, the term 'habitat' is generally used instead of biotope.

competition – The life activities of one species on one or more other species that depend on the same resources bring about competition between species (interspecific competition). Competition within a species (intraspecific competition) is usually a stronger force, as members of the same species require exactly the same resources in a single habitat. Competition can have two very different results. The clearly stronger (more vigorously competitive) species can prevail and force out the weaker one. But the weaker one often 'wins' when it is faster and more flexible in its use of resources.

contingency – an important term in history and evolutionary biology denoting relationships shaped in part by coincidence. Contingent processes can be traced and explained retrospectively according to the principle of cause and effect, but cannot be projected into the future in the same way. Just as contingent relationships alter the course of human history, they also influence evolution, the history of living things. It follows that ecology as concerned with the present can explain the composition of species diversity only against the background of natural history. Contingency thus always involves not only the physical-chemical laws of nature but also time as a determining factor in historical occurrences.

ecological factors – influences which cause changes in the environment

ecosystem – concept from the field of ecological research. On the basis of certain research questions, parts of nature – for example, a section of forest, a lake created by a dam, or a cultivated field – are demarcated and examined with regard to important processes such as metabolism of substances, passage of energy, or internal formation of structures. Demarcation is carried out according to research considerations, not naturally determined as in the case of an organism. Ecosystems are always open systems that lack three fundamental characteristics of organisms: the distinction between within and without, central control of internal processes, and the ability to reproduce. With its recent widespread currency and generalized use in everyday language, the term has come to be used almost arbitrarily. Ecosystems have no rigid, fixed states. They therefore cannot, contrary to wording common in nature protection literature, be 'stressed' or, much less, 'collapse.' Such formulations express the expectations or perspectives of humans and not objective conditions in nature. As a scientific term, 'ecosystem' combines the view of ecology developed in the late nineteenth century by German biologist Ernst Haeckel as 'the study of nature's metabolism' with the modern conception of systems dating to the 1950s.

endemic species – a species that occurs only in one particular area of the earth, making it a 'special resident' there. Endemic species are found especially on oceanic islands. Areas with very high biodiversity are also usually home to high numbers of endemic species. Endemic species frequently occur only in very small numbers and for this reason are especially vulnerable. The preservation of endemic species is the top priority of global species protection efforts.

food chains, food webs – sequences of nourishment in living nature beginning with the production of green plants or plant waste and proceeding by way of 'eating and being eaten' to the end consumer, the large predators or humans. Such a food chain may begin, for example, in the mud of a lake bottom, where bacteria and fungi consume organic waste material (detritus), forming microbial proteins that are ingested by tubifex worms (sludge worms) or the larvae of water insects. These are eaten by smaller fish, which in turn feed larger fish or waterfowl. The end of the 'chain' is reached with large predatory fish, ospreys, or fishermen. Usually food chains are interconnected in food webs.

gene flow – see subspecies

Holocene – see Pleistocene

ice age – an expression often ambiguously used for the geological era of the Pleistocene ('the Ice Age') or for the cold stages during this era. The last ice age was the cold stage variously called the Würm glaciation (the Alps), the Weichsel glaciation (Northern Europe), and the Wisconsin glaciation (North America). It ended roughly ten thousand years ago. Within the glacial epoch, however, the major cold stages have alternated with periods of pronounced warmth. The last of these, some one hundred twenty thousand years ago, was so warm that hippopotamuses inhabited the rivers of Northwestern Europe.

industrial melanism – increased occurrence of dark-colored individuals (melanistic mutants) in species, especially of butterflies, inhabiting regions with high levels of air pollution due to soot from industrial sources. This phenomenon, which demonstrates how rapidly evolution can take place, occurred above all in the nineteenth and the first half of the twentieth century.

life form – an animal or plant that is clearly distinct in kind from other living things, and can usually be identified as and assigned to a particular species quite different in appearance and life style from others. Certain life forms 'substitute' for one another on different continents as a result of long geological periods of separation. For example, as a plant eater of the steppe and semi-desert, the great kangaroo of Australia corresponds to goats, sheep, and some African and Asian antelopes. As it refers to external characteristics, 'form' stands in contrast to function. Often the form of a living thing shows what life conditions it is adapted to.

niche, ecological – ordinarily thought of as the 'place' a species takes or should take in nature. Scientifically, however, the term refers to the manifold relationships of a certain species of animals or plants to its environment. These cannot be limited to a fixed place or a certain 'corner' of nature. What a species 'can do' therefore is not entirely dependent upon where it lives at a given time. Many species have been able to enter into environments shaped by humans, sometimes inhabiting these even more successfully than their native biotopes. One such species is the Eurasian blackbird, a once shy and relatively rare forest bird that in just a few decades has become a very common and familiar urban resident. The numerous pests that harm crops and livestock are further examples.

Pleistocene – glacial epoch that began some two million years ago and ended (from our human perspective!) roughly ten thousand years ago. In all probability, the geological present, called the Holocene, is merely an interglacial period which will be followed by another cold period ('ice age' in the narrower sense).

Ruderal–a plant species which is the first to colonize an area of land disturbed by natural or manmade means, for example wildfire or avalanch; mining or building work.

species – a group of animals or plants whose individual members can breed with one another and reproduce over subsequent generations. For example, all house (English) sparrows comprise one species, even though, partly due to direct human influence, they are spread over most of the globe and those that inhabit North America have no contact with their European kin. In contrast, the quite similar Eurasian tree sparrow is clearly distinct from the house sparrow and makes up a separate species. All humans also belong to a single species, Homo sapiens. The first, capitalized term of a scientific name refers to the genus to which various further species may belong, or may have belonged in the past, such as Homo, our own genus, which included the Neanderthal. The second term, always lower case, is the species name: sapiens for our human species, neanderthalensis for our extinct Ice Age cousin. Conclusively distinguishing between species is often difficult, since only where two very similar species occur together (sympatrically) without intermixing do we have natural (biological) proof of their independence. When two similar groups of a single genus are separated by geography, without the opportunity to come together and breed, it takes scientific experimentation to ultimately establish whether they are different species or merely two subspecies. The fact that this is not possible with extinct species further contributes to the difficulty of species definition.

subspecies – definable subgroup within a species, inhabiting a certain geographic area and distinguishable from other subgroups of the species by recognizable characteristics. Evolutionary separation of the subspecies from the common ancestor is not yet so advanced as to preclude successful mating across this division, yet a high degree of isolation effectively keeps this from taking place. Gene flow is thus strongly restricted or prevented.

succession – sequence of stages in the development of a habitat following its colonization. Change occurs rapidly in the early stages. The longer the succession continues, the longer the stages become, until a kind of final, climax state is reached. This too can break down, however, setting in motion a new succession cycle. For example, when an agricultural area in Central Europe is left uncultivated, numerous stages of succession will give rise to a forest that will then remain for a long period.

Tertiary – 'third' geologic period, which followed the Paleozoic and Mesozoic eras, beginning some 65 million years ago and continuing to the advent of the glacial epoch (Pleistocene). By far the greatest part of the variety of life on the planet today dates from the Tertiary. The greatest richness of life on earth was reached during certain especially warm periods of the Tertiary.

variety of species – the number of animal and/or plant species in an area or region. The scientific term is species diversity. To avoid monotony of expression, variety of species is often used interchangeably with species richness. In a stricter sense, however, species richness is used with respect to certain designated sections of terrain. Thus even if the variety of species in the entire region is very high, the species richness per square kilometer may be only moderate if the different species tend to inhabit distinct adjoining areas rather than overlapping ones. Ecological researchers derive important basic facts from the relationship between general variety of species in an area and species richness per unit of area – for example, that a given habitat shows only limited productivity. Variety of species is often used in the field of nature conservation as a key criterion in the 'assessment' of an area.

References

The references listed here are a very personal selection. Given the vast number of publications on species and nature protection, it is impossible to compile even the most important ones, as different perspectives necessarily result in different choices. I welcome anyone who believes certain works or they themselves have not been considered appropriately to contact me so that I can correct and round out this list. I will be happy to do so. Publications particularly suitable for complementing this book and providing more depth are highlighted in **bold** print. Since this list of references includes books of mine, I have not needed to quote my own sources extensively. Some renowned textbooks of whose exceptional quality the author is convinced are given for readers interested specially in the ecological fundamentals. I intentionally decided not to quote from specialist journals so as not to discourage readers from using this list of references.

Bauer, Hans Günter and Peter Berthold. 1995. *Die Brutvögel Mitteleuropas. Bestand und Gefährdung.* Wiesbaden: Aula.

Bayerische Akademie der Wissenschaften. 2001. *Gebietsfremde Arten, die Ökologie und der Naturschutz. – Rundgespräch 22 der Kommission für Ökologie.* Munich: Pfeil.

Bayerische Akademie der Wissenschaften. 2003. *Biologische Vielfalt: Sammeln, Sammlungen und Systematik. –*

Rundgespräch 24 der Kommission für Ökologie. Munich: Pfeil.

Bayerisches Landesamt für Umweltschutz (ed.). 2003. *Rote Liste gefährdeter Gefäßpflanzen Bayerns mit regionalisierter Florenliste. – Schriftenreihe Heft 165.*

Bayerisches Landesamt für Umweltschutz (ed.). 2003. *Rote Liste gefährdeter Tiere Bayerns. – Schriftenreihe Heft 166.*

Bezzel, Einhard, Ingrid Geiersberger, Günter von Lossow and Robert Pfeifer. 2005. *Brutvögel in Bayern.* Stuttgart: Ulmer.

Dobson, Andrew P. 1996. *Conservation and Biodiversity.* New York: Scientific American.

Gleich, Michael, Dirk Maxeiner, Michael Miersch and Fabian Nicolay. 2002. *Life Counts. Cataloguing Life on Earth.* Atlantic Monthly Press.

Goldammer, Johann G. 1993. *Feuer in den Waldökosystemen der Tropen und Subtropen.* Basel: Birkhäuser.

H. R. H. Prince Philip. 1988. *Down to Earth.* London: Collins.

Hahlbrock, Klaus. 2009. *Feeding the Planet: Environmental Protection through Sustainable Agriculture.* London: Haus Publishing.

Hobohm, Carsten. 2000. *Biodiversität.* Heidelberg: Quelle & Meyer.

Kaufmann, Les and Kenneth Mallory (eds.). 1986. *The Last Extinction.* Cambridge, MA: MIT Press.

Kaule, Giselher. 1986. *Arten- und Biotopschutz.* Stuttgart: Ulmer.

Kellert, Stephan and Edward O. Wilson. 1993. The *Biophilia Hypothesis.* Washington, DC: Island Press.

Küster, Hansjörg. 1996. *Geschichte der Landschaft in Mitteleuropa.* Munich: C. H. Beck.

Küster, Hansjörg. 1998. *Geschichte des Waldes.* Munich: C. H. Beck.

Küster, Hansjörg. 2005. *Das ist Ökologie*. Munich: C. H. Beck.

Leakey, Richard and Roger Lewin. 1995. *The Sixth Extinction. Patterns of Life and the Future of Humankind*. New York: Doubleday.

Luard, Nicholas. 1981. *The Last Wilderness*. New York: Simon and Schuster.

MacArthur, Robert H. and Edward O. Wilson. 1967. *The Theory of Island Biogeography*. Princeton, NJ: Princeton University Press.

Magurran, Anne E. 1988. *Ecological Diversity and its Measurement*. London: Chapman and Hall.

Martin, Konrad. 2002. *Ökologie der Biozönosen*. Berlin: Springer.

Mowat, Farley. 1984. *Sea of Slaughter*. Toronto: McLelland and Stewart.

Myers, Norman (1985): *The Sinking Ark*. Synergism.

Odum, Eugene P. and Josef H. Reichholf. 1980. *Ökologie*. Munich: BLV.

Ott, Wilfried. 2004. *Die besiegte Wildnis*. Leinfelden-Echterdingen: DRW Weinbrenner.

Owens, Delia and Mark. 1992. *Survivor's Song*. London: Harper Collins.

Owen-Smith, R. Norman. 1988. *Megaherbivores*. Cambridge: Cambridge University Press.

Plachter, Harald. 1991. *Naturschutz*. Stuttgart: Ulmer.

Primack, Richard and Richard Corlett. 2005. *Tropical Rain Forests*. Oxford: Blackwell.

Primack, Richard B. 2006. *Essentials of Conservation Biology*. Sunderland, MA: Sinauer Associates.

Reichholf, Josef H. 1990. *Der Tropische Regenwald*. Munich: dtv.

Reichholf, Josef H. 2004. *Der Tanz um das goldene Kalb. Der Ökokolonialismus Europas*. Berlin: Wagenbach.

Reichholf, Josef H. 2005. *Die Zukunft der Arten*. Munich: C. H. Beck.

Reichholf, Josef H. 2007. *Stadtnatur*. Munich: Oekom.

Remmert, Hermann. 1980. *Arctic Animal Ecology*. Berlin: Springer.

Remmert, Hermann. 1988. *Naturschutz*. Berlin: Springer.

Remmert, Hermann. 1980. *Ecology*. Berlin: Springer.

Ricklefs, Robert E. 2008. *The Economy of Nature*. New York: WH Freeman.

Ricklefs, Robert E. 1979. *Ecology*. New York: Chiron Press.

Rosenzweig, Michael L. 1995. *Species diversity in space and time*. Cambridge: Cambridge University Press.

Schaller, George B. 1993. *The Last Panda*. Chicago: Chicago University Press.

Scherzinger, Wolfgang. 1996. *Naturschutz im Wald*. Stuttgart: Ulmer.

Schroeder, Fred-Günter. 1998. *Lehrbuch der Pflanzengeographie*. Heidelberg: Quelle & Meyer.

Terborgh, John. 1992. *Diversity and the Tropical Rain Forest*. New York: W. H. Freeman & Co.

Wilson, Edward O. (ed.) 1988. *Biodiversity*. Washington, DC: National Academy Press.

Wilson, Edward O. (ed.) 1992. *The Diversity of Life*. Cambridge, MA: Belknap Press of Harvard University Press.

Wittig, Rüdiger and Bruno Streit. 2004. *Ökologie*. Stuttgart: Ulmer.

Wittig, Rüdiger. 1991. *Ökologie der Großstadtflora*. Stuttgart: G. Fischer.

Credits

All diagrams: Peter Palm, Berlin, following Reichholf (unless stated otherwise in the legend). Color photographs: Fig. IV: G. Mayer; Fig. V (left): picture-alliance/dpa/kina; Fig. XIX: J. Diller; Fig. XXIV: picture-alliance/Klett GmbH; Fig. XXV: M. Unsöld; the other photographs are from the author's archive (with the exception of Figs. VIII and X).